GALLERY OF MODERN ART
GLASGOW

GALLERY OF MODERN ART GLASGOW

The First Years

SCALA BOOKS

First published in 1996 by Scala Books
an imprint of
Philip Wilson Publishers Ltd
143–149 Great Portland Street
London W1N 5FB

ISBN 0 902752 53 7

Design by Andrew Shoolbred with Newton Harris
Edited by Christopher Baker
Printed and bound in Italy by Sfera International, Milan

Acknowledgements

Glasgow Museums thank all the artists who kindly gave permission to reproduce illustrations of their works in this book.

The production of this publication owes a great deal to the many artists who contributed a personal statement about their work; the sponsors of the gallery; Deborah McCreadie for her research assistance and the dedicated, enthusiastic staff of Glasgow Museums.

This book contains selected highlights of the modern collection and does not attempt to represent its full diversity.

The dimensions of all paintings and works of art are given in centimetres, unless stated otherwise, and presented as height x width.

European Regional Development Fund

Frontispiece

John Bellany
The Ventriloquist 1983

Opposite page

Victor Tiede
How the West was Wild 1992

Contents

Sponsor's Statement

'Much of the treasure of the city'

The Royal Bank of Scotland opened for business in Glasgow in 1783. By 1800 the branch was the biggest banking operation outside London.

These were the years when the Bank financed trade with new markets such as the West Indies, made ingenious developments not only in engineering and textiles, but also canal building and railways, and with a host of smaller customers, maltmen and tallow chandlers, hocksters and glewmakers, qualifiers of tobacco and lint-hecklers, change-keepers and inkle-makers.

Sponsorship of the Earth Gallery, housed in the building we occupied from 1817 to 1827, allows us to recall those early days.

When the city's fashionable and wealthy were lured westward to what had been cow pastures, the Royal Bank had followed them and bought the substantial mansion built by tobacco tycoon William Cunninghame. It was a move that helped shift the city's financial centre of gravity to its present busy headquarters and offices.

The ten years we spent there were eventful ones. In 1820, with political agitation at its height, the mansion-branch was, observed one Glasgow historian, 'carefully Barricaded all around because it contained much of the treasure of the city; in fact the Royal Bank might then be represented to be as the Mint of the Tower of Glasgow.'

The fears of the City Fathers proved unfounded. There was no Glasgow Revolution and Captain Smith's Sharpshooters defending the bank were not called upon to use the 20 rounds of ball cartidges in their cartouches.

Today, it is good to see 'much of the treasure of the City', if a very different treasure, back in the mansion. And good that we have helped make it happen.

Lord Younger of Prestwick
Chairman, The Royal Bank of Scotland

7

David Hockney
Photography is Dead, Long Live Painting 1995
PHOTOGRAPH
83 x 104cm

Director's Preface

Welcome to Glasgow's Gallery of Modern Art. It is the dream of many a curator to open a new museum, but very few ever even think of starting a new collection. This gallery is a new museum and a new collection, and we hope you will find it beautiful and welcoming.

This is only the beginning of a collection: it will grow and change over the years in many ways that we cannot predict. What we have tried to do is to lay good foundations for its future growth. This has meant asking some fundamental questions about the role of modern art in society today, such as what criteria can be used to select the art that goes in the gallery, and what separates good art from bad? Not only have we had to ask these questions, but we have had to propose answers to them. This gallery represents the beginning of that process.

But before I start to describe and explain what we have done, I would like to make a personal tribute: to Glasgow. During my interview for the job of Director of Glasgow Museums in 1988, I mentioned that we needed more money to buy modern art. After I had been in the post eight months, the Leader of the Council, Councillor Pat Lally, called me into his office and said, 'You said you needed more money for buying modern art – would three million pounds do?' I was too surprised to reply.

'You can't spend it all at once,' he told me, 'but we'll put it into a fund and you can use the interest. Over the years you'll be spending much more than three million. It'll be a long term benefit from 1990 onwards. Do you want any conditions put on it?'

I immediately said, 'I only want one: that it is used to acquire art by living artists.' I did not want it to get gobbled up by the art market, which values art more for its investment potential than its aesthetic content. Concentrating on living artists would also naturally determine the time-frame of the gallery. In addition it would mean that we could talk to them about why they do what they do, and so put their art into context – which I think is vital in gaining the interest of a wider audience.

I did not want to limit the collection to Scottish artists. There is after all some difficulty in defining who is a Scot; for example, how do you distinguish the Scottishness of someone who was born here but subsequently left, and someone born elsewhere who came here to live? My view was that the gallery would be naturally based in Glasgow and Scotland, but that it should also represent the art of the world. Like Glasgow itself, the gallery has both to have its own identity and to take part in the world, to be both national and international in ambition and scope. The gallery will be doing its job well if it can bring Glasgow's art to the world and the world's art to Glasgow.

So the fund was established. Then I said, 'Now we're acquiring all this modern art, we'll have to find somewhere to show it.' The Royal Exchange building is an excellent location for the gallery – right in the heart of the city – because, quite simply, I think art is in the heart of Glasgow. Glaswegians are naturally cultured people – it would never occur to them that art was elitist, it is just part of life. A brief chat with almost any taxi driver in the city will confirm this. Of course, you do not have to like everything that is put before you. You are expected to have feelings – and what is art but the expression of feelings? Glasgow is naturally artistic and naturally egalitarian. What better place for a Gallery of Modern Art?

I cannot tell you what a relief it was to discover these qualities after years of living and working in England where, I believe, class divisions still dominate taste and weaken the role of art. It used to be said in the nineteenth century that English art students could draw while the Scots could paint. There is still a lot of truth in this. Art is more full-blooded here, though the pool is smaller. A hint of what I mean can be got from comparing the art of, say, David Hockney, with that of John Bellany or, to go back a generation, that of Patrick Heron with Alan Davie, or John Bratby with Joan Eardley. It is this painterliness, this broadly based, vigorous, natural artistic talent to which I want to pay a personal tribute, because it has provided the basis for this gallery. It has also given me the confidence to express what I believe is good about art.

This gallery is to some extent an expression of commitment. It is only a beginning; I have attempted to root it well in national and international artistic creativity. But I would not have been able even to start had it not been for the Council's magnificent response to my initial plea, and its subsequent determination to open the gallery in the heart of the city. This is politics at its most imaginative, giving expression to people's fuller aspirations – the natural creativity of Glasgow.

Julian Spalding

Director, Glasgow Museums

The Story of the Building

Stefan van Raay
Senior Curator of Art, Glasgow Museums

One of the most splendid houses then built in the West of Scotland.

Before 1776, Queen Street and Ingram Street were still rural routes from and to the city of Glasgow: Cow Lane and Back Cow Lane, respectively. The townsmen's cattle were conducted by these routes to the feeding ground on the Cowcaddens by the old town herdsman with his horn and cudgel, and under the hooves of his many beasts the two routes were more of a quagmire than a road. A dilapidated farmstead with its thatched stables and byres stood on the spot where the Gallery of Modern Art stands now. However, the prosperity of the tobacco merchants caused an expansion of the city westwards, with the subsequent development over-whelming these rural pursuits.

Walter Nelson, the owner of the land between St Enoch's Gate and the west side of Cow Lane, laid out Ingram Street and Queen Street in 1776 (naming the latter after Queen Charlotte) and sold the land as building plots (page 13). Ingram Street was later described as 'the spine of Glasgow's New Town, originally closed to the High Street and termi-nated to the west by a very handsome building with an open court and wings, adorned with all the ornaments that Grecian architecture can bestow.' This handsome building was the mansion of William Cunninghame, one of the Tobacco Lords of Glasgow.

In 1749, aged 18, William Cunninghame travelled from his native Ayrshire to America to begin his mercantile career. After his return he became one of the most successful tobacco merchants in the city. In 1763 Cunninghame married the daughter of another merchant, and he was so proud of his own achievements that he stip-ulated that should only a daughter be born to them, she should marry someone also called Cunninghame – to continue his family name.

The new rich, such as Cunninghame, were keen to uphold what they perceived as the same values as the long-established landed gentry of Glasgow. He expressed his status as one of the four richest Tobacco Lords of the city in his new mansion on Queen Street. It was described as follows:

> On the ground thus first acquired, Mr Cunninghame built, soon after 1778, one of the most splendid houses then built in the West of Scotland. It is said to have cost £10,000. It stood back from the street and consisted of three storeys, with wings placed at right angles to the mansion, and facing each other. A parapet wall ran along the street, with two iron gates on the north and south ends, and the large area in front of the house was covered with gravel. Behind the mansion was a garden with Jargonella trees trained along the wall.

The architect of this 'most splendid' house is not known, but he was certainly aware of the Palladian style then so popular in Britain. Palladian elements included the classical pilasters and pediments above the first floor windows, the balustrade at the top of the house, and the pediment on the main frontage with the Cunninghame crest. The frieze underneath it read: 'Emergo' (I emerge).

The plans of 1778 (page 12) show a semi-circular extension to the house at the garden side, probably a space for a grand staircase or salon. Half of it was preserved as a lobby to the main hall by David Hamilton, the later architect most readily associated with the building.

Today one can find several remains of the Cunninghame mansion (page 13) within the Gallery of Modern Art; the entrance hall, the ellipse with the rooflight, and the mansion house galleries on the first floor all echo the eighteenth-century plan. The modern public staircase and lift divide two large rooms on the south side of the house, on the ground and first floors, the latter being the former drawing-room.

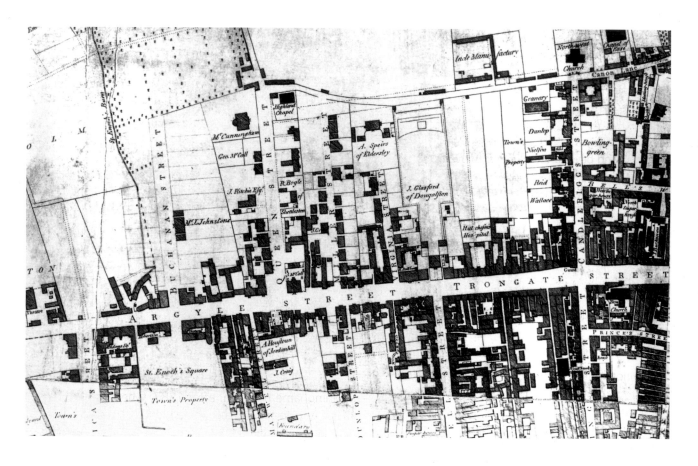

John McArthur's plan of the City of Glasgow 1778

Here the expansion of the city westwards can be seen, showing the mercantile villas along Miller Street and Queen Street, among them Mr Cunninghame's, at the top of Queen Street at the left side.
Courtesy of the Trustees of the National Library of Scotland.

In 1789, John Stirling, a descendant of one of the oldest families in Glasgow, bought the house and lived there privately, although the family business was run from one of the wings. His sons sold the house to the Royal Bank of Scotland in 1817 – a sign that this suburban area of the city was being transformed into a central business district. The bank commissioned, after 1827, the architect Archibald Elliot II to prepare plans for a new bank building to the west side of the old mansion house, where it stands today, and for terraces of shops and business chambers on the north and south sides of the square.

In 1827 the Royal Bank of Scotland sold Cunninghame's mansion to a consortium of city magistrates, merchants and manufacturers, to enable an Exchange to be built. The new Exchange, in the middle of the redesigned square – now named Royal Exchange Square – had to provide space for many activities. It included a news room, reading room, underwriters' rooms and bankers' offices, sugar, cotton and other sample rooms, and a general exhibition room, lit for the occasional display of paintings.

The use of the new square was strictly regulated. The Exchange Committee decided that the new buildings on the north and the south sides should not be used for anything considered 'offensive', such as butchers' or fishmongers' premises, or the selling of vegetables, ham, cheese, oil or tallow. Signs were strictly regulated – nothing was to extend beyond the plane of the walls, so as not to ruin the elegance of the square. The result was a beautifully proportioned example of civic planning.

The design was commissioned from the architect David Hamilton (1768–1843), and he incorporated the old mansion house within his building, encasing it between a new giant portico at the front and the main hall at the back. The consortium was apparently quite content with the plans, because when the foundation stone was laid on 20 December 1827, the secretary praised them highly:

> I do not hesitate to predict that the time is approaching when the work which we have just commenced will be hailed as an era in the annals of our community, and will be pronounced a credit to the projectors, a benefit to the public and an ornament to the city. Look at the mansion before you – and when the colonnade and portico in front are completed, will anything be more elegant? Look at the plans of the whole structure in the hands of the architect, and now exhibited before you – can anything be more beautiful? In short, ornament with simplicity, splendour with convenience, utility with taste.

Two years later, in 1829, the Exchange was officially opened.

The new frontage with the giant Corinthian portico – a perfect exercise in neo-classical architecture – surmounted by the tower, was exceptionally effective as the focal point at the west end of Ingram Street (page 14). Inside, Hamilton's main hall with its splendid Corinthian columns and barrel vault ceiling was the most imposing feature of the building. This was the news room, used for general business purposes in the new Royal Exchange.

After expenditure in excess of £50,000 the building was ready for use, and stayed at the heart of Glasgow's business community for more than one hundred years, at first mainly for trade in commodities like tobacco, sugar, rum and molasses,

The Cunninghame mansion, after 1887, when the staircase to the first floor was added

Picture, Royal Commission on the Historical Monuments of Scotland. Courtesy of *Scotland's Magazine*.

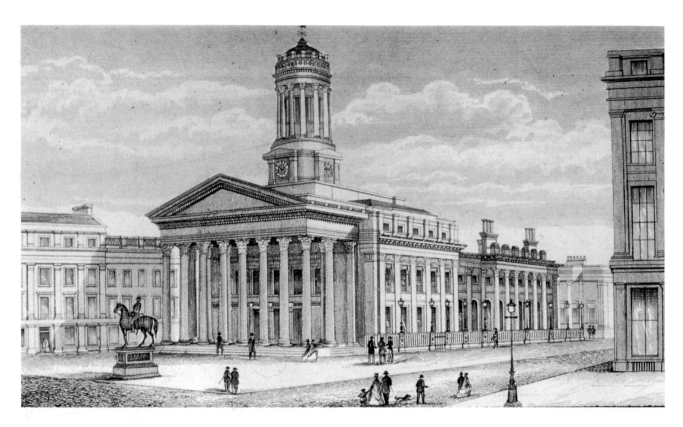

The new Royal Exchange from the north east, pre 1872

From *Glasghu Facies* by James F. S. Gordon

and later pig iron, coal and shipping. The Exchange provided all kinds of facilities. In 1828 a coffee tavern was opened in the basement, called the Crown Royal Exchange Tavern as a compliment to King William IV; a smoking room, barbers' shop and post office were also established, and in 1869 telegraphic equipment was installed. In 1889 a mansard roof was added to provide space for additional offices and to house Glasgow's first telephone exchange.

The Royal Exchange was used not only for business, but also formed a splendid setting for grand festive occasions, such as the ball held on 10 March 1863 to mark the marriage of the Prince of Wales, later Edward VII, to Princess Alexandra of Denmark. It was also used to entertain visiting dignitaries to the city, the guest list including kings, prime ministers, ambassadors, writers and many, many others.

The members of the Exchange organized or supported social and sporting events. In 1924, for example, a silver golfing trophy – a replica of the *Warwick Vase* – was presented by the Exchange to be competed for annually by members (the *Warwick Vase* itself is now part of The Burrell Collection).

The last major remodelling within the building occurred in 1913 when, under the architect Colin Menzies, the old walls in the basement, which supported the huge columns in the main hall, were replaced by square pillars. These pillars and the walls were covered with marble, the whole basement becoming a restaurant. After World War II, the City of Glasgow bought the Royal Exchange for £105,000, and in 1949 the Stirling Library was moved into it from its original premises in Miller Street. The Library was named after the merchant Walter Stirling who, in 1791, had left his house in Miller Street and his collection of books to the city, with the intention of creating and maintaining a public library. This library was merged with other libraries in the nineteenth century and its name is all that remains to remind us of Stirling's enlightened gesture. Those Glaswegians who used the library in Royal Exchange Square will remember passing only through the elliptical entrance hallway with its curved doors into the main hall, furnished with desks and bookcases, as the rest of the building had been out of use for many years.

When the Library returned to premises in Miller Street in 1994, the conversion programme was begun, so that the building could house the city's modern art collections. The Department of Architecture and Related Services and the Museums Department decided to retain as many features of the historic building as possible, both externally and internally. This was difficult sometimes, because of present-day requirements, such as lifts and suitable public stairs. Details like floors, wall finishes and ceilings had to be adapted to the new use as a public gallery whilst retaining the character of the many distinctive spaces. The additions of a café on the roof and the pyramidal rooflights in the Air Gallery are major changes that have been made to the building.

The main features of the former Royal Exchange survive within the Gallery of Modern Art: Earth Gallery – main hall; Fire Gallery – basement; Air Gallery – mansard roof space. The Water Gallery on the first floor has been achieved by removing the divisions which created the office spaces.

The Gallery of Modern Art has a rich historic past. An equally important future stretches ahead, providing interest and enjoyment of the visual arts for the people of Glasgow and the city's welcome visitors.

Interior of the main hall of Stirling's Library, 1954

Courtesy of Glasgow Libraries

Bibliography

Bewsher, C. C., *The Centenary of the Royal Exchange, Glasgow*, Glasgow, 1927, p.26.

Eyre-Todd, G., 'Romance of Glasgow Streets', in *Glasgow Scrapbooks*, no. 17, 1935, p.237.

McKean, C., Walker, D. and Walker, F., *Central Glasgow*, RIAS, 1993, p.71.

Tweed, J., *Glasgow Ancient and Modern*, Glasgow, 1872, p.1054.

Art for People

Julian Spalding
Director, Glasgow Museums

Ken Currie's *The Bathers* (below) and Peter Howson's *Patriots* (opposite) are paintings about man's inhumanity to man. I can think of few artists who have taken on such an ambitious subject so successfully since the last war. The very idea of public painting with a serious purpose has gone out of fashion in recent years. This is partly because painting itself has had a hard time competing with modern communication media, like photography and video, and recently computer-generated imagery, which are all reproducible and can, therefore, meet our myriad needs. By comparison with them, painting seems anachronistic – an old craft incompatible with mechanical reproduction; but the fact that it is hand-made gives painting its advantage. It means every inch of it has gone through someone's mind, whereas most of a photo-graph has only gone through a machine. Only a very great photographer, like Sebastião Salgado, can make a photograph look like a painting, as if he had meant it all and imbued it all with feeling, whereas a painting cannot help but be a statement of a personal position.

This gallery proclaims the importance of personal experience in art. The sheer number of people everywhere and the unimaginable scale of the macrocosm and the microcosm that scientists have discovered argue against the significance of the individual. But what do 5,722 million of us have but our individual experiences? When Bishop Berkeley in the eighteenth century claimed that all material things were an illusion, Dr. Johnson replied, 'I refute that, sir, by this' – and he stubbed his foot on a stone. Art is about personal experience. John

Ken Currie

The Bathers 1992–3

OIL ON LINEN

259 x 420cm

With the conflict of Bosnia uppermost in his mind, Currie developed this picture from a dream, as 'a warning against the re-emergence of xenophobia, and racial and religious intolerance at a time when extreme nationalism and racist ideas appear to be flourishing in the vacuum created by the collapse of the communist regimes.'

Peter Howson

Patriots 1991

OIL ON CANVAS

206 x 275cm

'In 1991 I was walking through Gallowgate in Glasgow one morning. Across the road I saw three men running with two dogs. Both man and dog were aggressively posturing when they stopped, and then continued to run. The men wore baseball caps and shell suits. I only saw them for a few seconds but it left a strong impression on me.

'I worked on about twenty preliminary drawings and then I painted. I transported the figures from the city to a bleak cliff landscape. The painting is about Britain and its obsession with machismo and patriotism. I wanted the paintings to capture the atmosphere of the late '80s and early '90s with its random violence, great bigotry (the Patriots could come from any class) and moral confusion. The last refuge of a scoundrel is patriotism.'

Ruskin, the Victorian art critic, said that the artist's job is to see and to feel. The practice of art was not then in question. Now we have to add that the artist's job is not only to see and feel but to find an expressive language that enables others to see what the artist has felt. The traditional media – painting, sculpture, print-making and drawing – still have a great advantage over contemporary media, in that they are infinitely subtle and controllable.

One might have thought that everything that could be done had been done in painting when Leonardo created the *Mona Lisa* and Michelangelo painted the Sistine Ceiling – but who at that time could have predicted Vermeer or Turner, Van Gogh or Matisse? And so it will go on. Glasgow's collections contain a great deal of traditional art – particularly painting, which has developed strongly in Scotland over the last few years – simply because it can still say more than modern media, and will, I believe, have more to say in the future.

The idea that a painting may have something to say has become unfashionable, odd though this may seem to anyone outside the art world. If you ask someone in the art world what a work of art is about, you are likely to be thought naïve. Art, it is often asserted, is not about anything; it just is. This is nonsense: everyone knows existence is not possible in isolation. If a work of art is not about something, it must, then, be about nothing. This gallery unashamedly shows art that is about something.

Art that is about something still has to be art, otherwise, it would remain just a statement, an instruction or a direction, something that you might just as well think, and that there is no need to paint. Statements are not art because they lack feeling. Art gives form to feeling. Propaganda, because it arouses feelings, is the beginning of art and all art has some degree of propaganda in it. Look, for example, at the work of the Korean artist Hong Song-Dam (page 31). Even modern art that proclaims to be about nothing usually has some element of propaganda in it; its very obscurity is often a way of saying, 'Aren't I important?'.

Fear of being dismissed as propaganda is one reason why art has been so mute recently, why it has pretended it has nothing to say. This fear is a residue of recent political history. Both Hitler in Nazi Germany and, later, Khruschev in Communist Russia favoured realistic art that had a political message; their 'art for the people' looked like something and was about something. They therefore outlawed abstract and expressionist art. By contrast, America, during the Cold War, promoted the art that combined both these styles. It was appropriately called Abstract Expressionism (the action painting of Jackson Pollock is an example) and it became a symbol of freedom in American society.

Artists and promoters are still suffering from a nervousness about being representative and populist. They are suspicious of any art that claims to be 'for people'. Picasso never tried to paint a purely abstract picture; he was fond of saying that he always added a figurative element to his pictures, to give people a way into what the work was about. Ken Currie and Peter Howson are not

Peter Howson
Johnie 1987
ETCHING
33 x 24cm

Picassos; they have not re-invented a whole new creative language. In comparison with his achievement, they can, in some ways, be seen as reactionary. But they had to react – against the vacuousness of so much modern art – to reclaim for art a whole area of subject-matter and a whole area of language. Reclaiming the former required determined conviction, reclaiming the latter required sheer hard work. The art of figurative drawing, let alone painting, has been almost totally lost since the war, and it is not re-learned overnight. Given the circumstances of their time, their achievement to go back to the basics of figurative art – and learn to draw the figure again – is heroic.

The two key elements of drawing are line and shading. Line is the key to the power of *Patriots*, shading is the key to the power of *The Bathers*. Howson is one of the finest draughtsmen I know (opposite). How infinitely subtle and variable a mere line can be! Just compare Howson's work with that of other great British draughtsmen, like David Hockney and John Bellany. Hockney's line moves on the surface of the paper, like the tip of a tongue exploring the flesh of a lover, dipping here and there but always remaining concise and detached, on the surface, as an observer. John Bellany appears to search for his line with what are often at first very delicate strokes. Then, finding where the line is, he becomes confident and explores that seam of feeling, as in his *Self Portrait* (page 72).

Peter Howson's line could not be more different; at its best it is supremely confident, defining form as he determines character. There is a wonderful Scots word, thrawn, which relates to his work. It is applied to someone who has been strengthened by adversity, like a thorn tree on an exposed hillside which is beaten by strong winds and grows twisted and bent and all the tougher for it. Peter Howson sees people clearly, how they have grown to be what they are. He draws the lines that life has given them. Howson's paintings and drawings celebrate the struggle of individual lives. He often depicts this struggle as heroic, but he is haunted too by an awareness of how destructive people can become. *Patriots* is, I think, his most powerful expression of human aggression to date. In the late 1980s Howson saw and felt an emerging violence in people. It appeared on the political stage with the issue of the control of dangerous dogs. These were becoming increasingly popular pets among people

who espoused a bigoted form of British nationalism in the aftermath of the Falklands War. Howson saw these animals with their masters, and expressed his feelings about them in an image that will, I think, become one of the icons of its age. *Patriots* is a remarkable feat of draughtsmanship. Anyone who has tried to draw people leaping in the air knows how difficult it is to give them weight and substance and relate them to the space around them, without making them look ludicrous.

It is a sign of a good painting that everything works together, the spaces around objects as well as the spaces within them. Howson has articulated the whole composition like a dance. Everything moves together including, rather exceptionally for him, the brushwork, which flows freely around the forms, giving substance to the drawing. The men and their dogs are united in a movement that reminds one of the feeling when a crowd ceases to be a mass of individuals but acquires a life of its own, turns ugly and becomes an inhuman monster.

Ken Currie's *The Bathers* (page 16) explores a similar theme from a totally different viewpoint. His early works (such as his cycle of history paintings in the People's Palace, Glasgow) are paintings of hope. They are dark but they glow with light – a beam from a miner's helmet, or rays from a lantern in a clandestine trade union meeting or, as a pictorial device, as haloes of light that follow his dark lines everywhere, symbolizing the knowledge that has illuminated working people's lives over the centuries. Since the fall of the Berlin Wall and the defeat of Communism in the Soviet bloc, Currie's style has changed. His paintings have begun to explore many more shades of grey. He is a painter of gloom – the very word acquires new depths of meaning in his work.

Unlike any other equivalent painting by Currie, *The Bathers* was 'seen' by the artist in a dream as he explains:

The idea for this painting came around 1990. The starting point was a particularly vivid and harrowing dream. So powerful was the imagery that it stayed in my mind for many months. Prior to beginning to work I would have considered the notion of producing a large painting on something so fleeting and insubstantial as a dream as utter folly. However, the imagery and emotion aroused by this dream

John Bellany
Untitled

CRAYON

76 x 56cm

did, indeed, seem very concrete and tangible to the extent that an exploration seemed viable, if not, urgent. Consider the following description of the dream: I am walking down a familiar street in Glasgow. Suddenly a large ambulance pulls up and nurses appear everywhere. Not modern nurses but very severe, Victorian warden-like nurses. They all carry huge sheets with the Red Cross symbol on them. The ambulance positions itself at one side of the street and the nurses hold up the sheets to form a sort of corridor from the ambulance to the door of a large bath-house in a hospital, at the other side of the street. The doors of the ambulance open, as do the doors of the bath-house, where I see the usual steam, white tiles, pipes and so on. Figures begin to pour out of the ambulance and run along the corridor of sheets to the bath-house. By that time a large, leering, jeering crowd had gathered to watch. I am standing on the other side of this crowd, observing. Suddenly, there is a gust of wind and a nurse loses her grip on one of the sheets and it falls to the ground, revealing a sight of utter horror and pity – men, horribly maimed, crippled and diseased, covered in indescribable filth are running, crawling, limping to the bath-house. Their terror in being exposed in this way is painfully evident, but they continue their passage to the bath-house. I can hardly begin to describe the feeling I had on seeing them. One of the nurses shouts at me to lift the sheet back into place, which I do. Sensing my horror, she tells me that these men are extremely rare cases who live in total isolation in a remote colony, beyond all hope, abandoned, except for this moment – their annual bath. I continue to watch as the men enter the bath-house and, under the shower heads, cleanse themselves of their filth. They whoop with delight, dance with joy, embrace each other, look renewed and refreshed. The sense of relief is overwhelming. The feelings of shock evoked by this dream lingered for months.

Like all good art *The Bathers* is a complex, subtle and moving image – one that makes one want to go on looking at it and absorbing what it has to say for a long time. It makes a stand against the superficial dips into feeling that are provided for us by modern media, by its sheer scale, its laborious craftsmanship and its unrelenting, unapologetic concentration on its subject. Superficially it may look like a statement not of its time, but it is very much of its time. All it shows us is going on now – our ability to 'cleanse' from our thoughts and lives aspects of our nature which we do not want to face. Currie shows us things we do not want to see. Our age has given a whole new meaning to the verb 'to cleanse'. The Nazis told their Jewish victims that they were going into showers, when they were in fact going to be gassed. This was 'ethnic cleansing' as was the genocide in the former Yugoslavia that was going on at the time of writing. Currie adds to this litany of cleansing the way the better-off treat the poor, and the healthy treat the sick, and he sees in it our destructive aspirations to be other than we are. The language he has chosen to express these feelings is one borrowed from the old masters – the technique of chiaroscuro.

Light and shade are still fundamental to our lives. The vast natural resources we expend on dispelling the dark proves just how much we fear it, and just how much light gives us security and hope. Currie unveils fears and hopes in our superficially stable world, and he does so visually by using the power that light and shade have to move us. You must respond to the pictorial equivalents of these experiences – whiteness and blackness and the infinitely subtle range of tones in between if you are to feel the full force of this tragic painting. In his recent work Currie has shown a love of modulating light with dark, and dark with light – bruises stain pale flesh, shadows fall across searching eyes. In the West death is symbolized by black; in the East, by white. Only at the extremes is there nothingness. In between, light and dark flow through all our lives. Currie seems to be saying in this painting that it is how we face up to this that matters – and how terrible the consequences are when we try not to.

It is often thought that representational painting began to die when the camera was invented. To some people *The Bathers* looks naturalistic – but it could not be a photograph. This image has been created in the mind – and everything about it is thought and felt. As the impact of the discovery of photography weakens (and it is already being undermined by computer imaging), so painting will reclaim its full expressive domain – encompassing everything within its range from detailed representation to abstraction. 'Modern Art' is, I think, over. Art can now be modern without having to look 'modern', as Michael Sandle shows in his sculpture (page 91).

Who is to say that people in the future will not be more interested in the paintings of David Measures (page 87), than they are in the so-called big names in Modern Art who make so much money today. He has dedicated his life to painting the butterflies of Britain. David Measures does not kill his butterflies but paints them on the wing, with a spontaneity that makes his watercolours alive with them and the light they dance through. We love things as we lose them. Measures is an artist of our disappearing meadows and woodlands.

Every painting is abstract, in the sense that it is not real. The pipe in a painting is not a pipe – you cannot play on it. It is an abstraction of a pipe. Abstract art is still young and we are not yet used to looking at it in a picture. We are used to seeing it in our clothes, furnishings and buildings – but not in a frame. Frames for us are associated with windows or mirrors – we expect to see views through them. Looking at an abstract painting for many people is like opening the curtains to find the world has become a swirl of meaningless colours. To under-

Bridget Riley
Arrest III 1965
EMULSION ON LINEN
174 x 192cm

stand abstraction we have to forget about the windows and mirrors. This is one reason why abstract artists like Bridget Riley do not put frames on their paintings, Hock-Aun Teh makes his pictures irregular shapes, and Margaret Mellis makes reliefs and sculptures – so that they confront you as if you are meeting someone rather than opening a door through which you can see something.

Abstract art tends to come forward to meet you. Though it often has a great deal of space within it in, for instance, Francis Davison's collages of torn paper, abstract art tends to be assertive because it is still fighting to be accepted as art. It is, however, gaining ground, and many visitors to this gallery will, I am sure, have no difficulty looking at and enjoying the abstract as well as the figurative art. You will see that a linocut by Ken Currie and a painting by Bridget Riley (opposite) share the same basic visual language. What they have in common is that they are made by people who are using this language to communicate with you.

Art is made by people for people. Looking at a piece of art is like meeting a person. If you could not speak or write, how would you communicate? If you imagine as you go round this gallery that you are meeting people everywhere who cannot speak or write but are bursting to express what they have to say about their experience of the world, you will not go far wrong. Eduard Bersudsky (pages 49, 50) was so disturbed by what was happening around him in Communist Russia that he became an elective mute and made sculptures that moved. He is an exception. Many of the people who made the art here are extremely articulate, but they very rarely talk about what their pictures say. If they could express in words what the paintings say, they would not have needed to paint them. Art, then, expresses experiences we cannot, and should not, try to express in other ways.

Painting, like music, poetry and geometry, is an extension of our understanding, of our humanity, not an illustration of something we know by other means. Once we accept that, art becomes relevant, even vital, to our well-being, individually and socially.

Modern art has been developed in recent years in a hothouse, uncritical atmosphere. There has been much criticism from outside of course, but this has been interpreted from within as acclaim! Many of the middle-men of modern art – the teachers,

Ken Currie
Industrial Accident from *Story from Glasgow*
1989
LINOCUT ON PAPER
17 x 22cm

Sebastião Salgado
Refugee Camp at Korem, Ethiopia 1984
PHOTOGRAPHIC PRINT
51 x 41cm

curators, critics, dealers and collectors – who are sustained by their own mini-economy, and supported by public funding – have been constrained by the fear of getting it wrong. Their predecessors were wrong about Van Gogh and Matisse and Picasso, and they are frightened of making similar mistakes.

The history of the art of our age will be written when it is past. What we have to do is to remain open-minded and responsive to the art that is actually being produced today – across the whole spectrum of artistic activity. We have to look particularly for art that seems to spring naturally, without being forced, from a society and people's lives of which it is part. Such art has more chance of being truly modern, because it will be a real product of its age, of what it has been like to experience life today.

To have a genuine response requires courage – the courage of one's own convictions. This involves overcoming one's fear of being wrong, while admitting that one certainly will be, at least part of the time. This has meant beginning with our personal responses. We have started by asking: what does this art actually mean to us? If it means very little to me, how can I expect it to mean much to you? This has meant looking with interest at art that has already created its audience not within the art world but outside, among ordinary people – popular art like Beryl Cook's (pages 39, 40). This may lead art specialists to accuse us of being populist, but we believe that art's future depends on it being rooted broadly in society, not preserved within the conservatory of an elite.

Art has to develop a broad language, capable of embracing humour and tragedy, poetry and prose, the whole gamut of human experience. It is one of the ambitions of this gallery to help art achieve this, by showing the whole range of art and attracting the widest spectrum of people. We hope that painting will reassert itself as one of the great image-making languages of our age.

At the moment that crown still rests with photography. Sebastião Salgado has created some of the most telling images of our times. It is a tribute to Salgado's passion and patience that his best images look as though they are painted. It is not just that each is beautifully composed, it is that every aspect of the picture, every detail, seems to enhance the emotional impact of the whole. An

Sebastião Salgado
Gold Mining, Serra Pelada, Brazil 1986
PHOTOGRAPHIC PRINT
51 x 41cm

example is the patch of light indicating figures in the distance behind the woman in *Refugee Camp at Korem, Ethiopia* (opposite). Not only do they provide a detail exactly where it is needed to balance the composition of the right tone – light enough to balance the main areas of dark – but they also add to the emotional force of the image by hinting at a world beyond, which goes on repeating the experience of this mother and child. And look at the angle of the mother's head. It is set with the composure of a Raphael Madonna, but its gaze is not sweet: these eyes speak of dignity in suffering.

Salgado has not composed this picture; he did not go up to the woman and say, turn your head to the side a little, hold it there. What he has done is to see and feel the image in the first place, then he has altered his position to find the angle that brings out most of what he has seen. And he has had to do this without disturbing what he is looking at. This requires the utmost respect, humility and technical ability. It is almost as though Salgado lives inside his camera. The tiniest lapse in his concentration and feeling could mean losing everything. It is an activity sustained by a passionate love for people. It is the same love that draws him to places of suffering all over the world. He is one of the great recorders of

Henri Cartier-Bresson
Behind the Gare St. Lazare, Paris 1932
PHOTOGRAPHIC PRINT

our times, and has created in his output a world-wide picture of human feeling, discovering even in the most terrible circumstances our ability to survive and assert our right to live. There is extraordinary dignity even in the degradation of the Serra Pelada gold-mining scene (page 25). His work there, as elsewhere, can be seen as a remarkable pilgrimage in search of the human spirit. He speaks with real authority when he says 'we are all one people, we are all probably one man'.

I was going to write that Salgado is one of the greatest artists of our times, but I stopped short. His photograph of a mother and child is not his song only; it is also theirs. She and her culture have made this photograph. Salgado has taken it. This is why Henri Cartier-Bresson, the great documentary photographer of the earlier part of the twentieth century, and Salgado's master, considered photography to be a form of pocket-picking. You do not make a photograph, you take it. Significantly, in the last fifteen years Cartier-Bresson has abandoned photography and concentrated on drawing (opposite).

Photography is a mechanical process that can be governed but not totally controlled. It is a cast from nature, not a creation. There has been a great deal of interest in casting, lately, among modern artists. The masters of this have been Boyle Family (page 28). In their work, as in a photograph by Salgado, you feel that every detail has been placed there on purpose to tell the history of a place. Other artists have cast their own bodies, others again have cast objects – in one case, a whole house. My own view is that this interest in casting is a sign that artists want to return to figuration but cannot quite start actually creating things themselves. The limitation with casting is that it is a language that you cannot actually develop. It is easy to create an emotive image with a cast – all death masks and mummies have it – but it is impossible to develop that emotive impact. To do that you have to start creating for yourself.

We have tried in this gallery to show art that is a natural product of life. Aboriginal art is the oldest living art form in the world. Their painting is essentially what it was 40,000 years ago and it still serves the same role in their society. Aborigines are now reduced to a tiny number, and until the seventies some were constrained within reserves imposed on them by white settlers, without any consultation about or understanding of their relationship to the land. Their history of displacement has been poignantly recorded in Robert Campbell Jr's painting *Who Said You Could Fish Here* (page 30).

Art is an integral part of Aboriginal life. Traditional Aborigines do not work in our conventional sense; their role within their society is to keep alive their traditions, which they do by singing and dancing, telling stories and painting. At initiation ceremonies adolescents are given secret stories and signs about different aspects of their world. One may be given the stories of, say, the catfish or the kangaroo, and another, if he is much more important, the stories of the night sky. Their role within the Dreaming is to keep these stories alive. If they do not, the catfish or the night sky and all that is associated with them will die.

The equivalent to this in our society is those people who feel they have some sort of mission – who become interested in something, often early in life, and devote their whole lives to preserving and developing it. David Measures (page 87) is like this. So too are those people who become champions of our heritage, or become absorbed in areas of scientific research or social justice. It is often these people who through their dedication and strength of feeling change our society for the better. And it is an interesting question to ask yourself – what do you feel responsible for? Our society has no formal way of channeling this aspect of human nature, but the Aborigines have – to such an extent that these responsibilities are at the core of their lives and their culture. This is probably one reason for the high suicide rate among Aborigines who leave their society, particularly those who are imprisoned. Not being able to carry on their work leaves them with a meaningless life.

One reason why art plays such a central role in traditional Aboriginal life is that they have no written language. Painting is, in fact, a form of writing for them. Much of this is a secret language, only fully known to the initiated. However, certain aspects of every story can be told openly, and it is these that have been told to us and that we have recorded with the pictures. Though their art is secret and religious, Aborigines are happy to sell it after it has been used, to help promote their culture. But when they do so they give only elementary explanations for the uninitiated – like ourselves.

The Night Sky Dreaming (page 29) was painted

Henri Cartier-Bresson
Self Portrait 1992
DRAWING
23 x 17cm

Boyle Family

Kerb Study with Metal Edge (Glasgow) 1985

FOUND MATERIAL IN RESIN ON FIBREGLASS

183 x 183 x 12cm

Mark Boyle has explained that this is a limited random study: 'one of a series of random studies made on a pavement in Glasgow with the limiting requirement that each section had to include a piece of black kerb stone.'

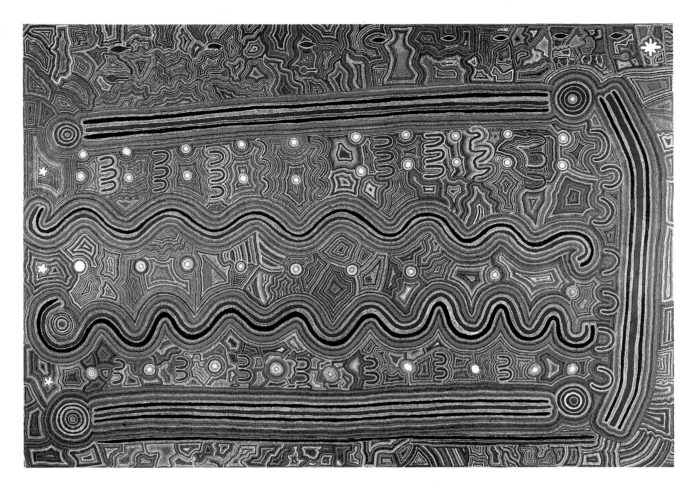

Paddy Japaljarri Sims
The Night Sky Dreaming 1993
ACRYLIC ON CANVAS
281 x 406cm

Paddy Japaljarri Sims with people from Yuendumu working on *The Night Sky Dreaming*

Photograph by Tamara Lucas

Robert Campbell Jr

Who Said You Could Fish Here 1988

ACRYLIC ON CANVAS

121 x 226cm

Felipe Linares at work in Mexico City

He says of his work: 'I inherited my calling from my father. Right from the start I liked the craft of papier mâché. It is an important Mexican tradition and I want to keep it alive – that is my motivation. It is very important to me that people are pleased with what I make.'

by Paddy Japaljarri Sims, together with other Aborigines – the Japaljarri and Jangarrayi men and the Napaljarri and Nungarrayi women, who jointly own the Dreaming (page 29) as part of the Night Sky Ceremony, which is re-enacted on a cycle of approximately twenty years, our time. They contacted us to say that they were going to do *The Night Sky Dreaming* and that they would like us to have the painting they produced during this ceremony after they had finished it. My colleague Tamara Lucas flew out to see the whole process.

In earlier times, *The Night Sky Dreaming* would have been painted on the ground, with coloured sands. It is painted throughout the ceremony which lasts in all about three weeks, as part of the story-telling, in between dancing and singing. This goes on through the day and night and many people come to see the ceremony. It is preceded by visits to the sacred sites recorded in the painting (because as well as stories, these pictures are also diagrammatic maps), and much star-gazing. Tamara told me that the men sat up all night. They were looking at the stars and telling stories about them. In the middle of the Australian desert, the night sky is totally clear; the stars fill it with light like a shimmering veil of opal. When Paddy Japaljarri Sims started work on the painting, he insisted that the canvas was painted all over first with a shockingly bright pink.

Tamara was distressed and asked him to stop. She was told to mind her own business and in the end, as dot after dot was added to the picture, the pink disappeared and the whole became exactly like the night sky she had seen. Without the pink underneath it could probably never have captured that remarkable luminescence. Looking at an Aboriginal painting closely reveals the delicacy and feeling with which each mark is made and the remarkably sophisticated colour sense.

Aboriginal painting has been enjoying a renaissance in recent years and must, I think, rank among the finest modern art today. Robert Campbell Jr's painting *Who Said You Could Fish Here* (opposite) uses the traditional artistic language of his own Aboriginal culture, but in the Western way of his adopted culture. He was one of those Aborigines who left his traditional way of life to live in the city, but then started painting scenes of his life to keep his and his people's history alive. This painting is representational and views the world from the side, as we do – not from above, as the Aboriginal artists do in their imagination. The effect of marrying the two approaches – Aboriginal markings and our perspective – is hallucinatory. We feel that everything in the landscape is moving, either growing like the fingers of the trees, or flowing like the river, or falling like the sky, or rising up like the arc of smoke from the fire. The Aborigines are doing what they have always done; but the white man has arrived to drive them off with his blindly arrogant question and his gun. For me, this whole landscape is crying.

One of the major challenges facing people today is to find a way to maintain their own cultural identity while becoming citizens of the world. It is one aspect of the struggle between nationalism and internationalism. People are becoming more interested in distant cultures, in 'world music' and world art. Vittorio Radice, Managing Director of Habitat UK, explained to me recently his world-wide buying policy: 'In Terence Conran's day, our customers went on their holidays to France, and they wanted to bring back something of the French country lifestyle into their homes. They now go on holidays around the world, and want to bring back something of that culture too.'

This demand has led to a tremendous growth in the production for tourists of traditional crafts, much of which is debased, imitative and uncreative. There is nothing wrong with this if it earns revenue

Hong Song-Dam
Resurrection 1989
WOODCUT
57 x 43cm

and gives pleasure, but we have looked for those visual arts that are still used by the people who make them, or which show traditional forms changing to reflect the new times we are living in. The Linares brothers, who make ephemeral painted *papier mâché* figures for the Day of the Dead ceremonies in Mexico (page 30), have taken contemporary themes on board in their work. Their art has naturally remained alive. There is no real difference between them being commissioned to make a group for a procession or for an art gallery, as we have invited them to do for our Gallery of Modern Art. They have chosen to make a sculpture of Death surrounded by modern versions of the Seven Deadly Sins. They will be the first artists-in-residence in what will be an on-going programme in the new gallery, aimed at bringing people who make art to people who look at art and, in the process, bringing the art itself to life.

The narrative woodcuts of Korea, which have a tradition dating back 1200 years, were the perfect vehicle for Hong Song-Dam (page 31) to express his horror at the atrocities in South Korea, and to rally support against it. He went on producing and distributing these prints, in spite of all attempts to stop him, until he was captured and imprisoned in 1989. Amnesty International called our attention to his plight – a man imprisoned because of the power of his art. War is a continuing reality in many borderline states; Salgado is of the opinion that the Third World War is happening now, along several fault lines around the world, and that it is aptly named.

Buka War (above) is an example of a war between government and local troops over international mining. Mathias Kauage comes from a culture in which war is ritualized. The highlands of Papua New Guinea are still peopled with small tribes who each have their own customs, terrains and language (half the languages of the world today are spoken in Papua New Guinea). Disputes between them are resolved by carefully ritualized battles which include a great deal of display –

Mathias Kauage
Buka War 1990
ACRYLIC ON CANVAS
122 x 173cm

Mathias Kauage
Suicide 1988
ACRYLIC ON CANVAS
96 x 67cm

Mathias Kauage
Carry Leg 1990
ACRYLIC ON CANVAS
98 x 93cm

painted shields, elaborate costumes, make-up and headdresses. Kauage's painting style springs directly from his own visual culture.

His designs are splayed, like his own headdress across the picture, to make the maximum impact. *Suicide* tells the story of a woman who, against her wishes, has given up her life of sexual freedom and agreed to the traditional marriage her parents have arranged for her. She is faithful to her husband but he is consumed with jealousy and constantly accuses her of being unfaithful to him. In despair she commits suicide in public by hanging herself from a tree in the forest. (Female suicide is a growing issue in Papua New Guinea.) Her husband, having discovered her, weeps at her feet. By contrast, *Carry Leg* is about a woman who defies her parents' pressure, refuses the husband they have arranged for her and lives in exuberant joy with her lover.

Kauage has developed a language that enables him to evoke tragedy and victory and give vivid expression to the personal consequences of a

Josef Szubert
The Harvest 1984
OIL ON HARDBOARD
46 x 56cm

Margaret Baird
School Days 1967
OIL ON HARDBOARD
33 x 44cm

society undergoing change. There is no tradition of easel painting in Papua New Guinea, so where did Kauage spring from?

He was a cleaner at the university where the German professor Ulli Beier taught literature, while his English wife Georgina painted. Knowing Georgina was a painter, Kauage brought her his drawings. They were copies of Western book illustrations. She did not like them and tried to persuade him not to go on bringing them to her. But he did. Then one day she noticed some little insects he had drawn in a quite different style. She said she liked them, and her interest opened up a floodgate of drawings from Kauage, then paintings, until gradually his whole new style emerged. He had developed a language that enabled him to express his feelings about much of what was happening in Papua New Guinea. Murals by him now decorate the government buildings there. People who have something to say are naturally eager to find people who will listen.

The story of art is the story of people interacting with people, which they do within the context of the society in which they live. Much has been written about this wider context of art, but the personal interactions that trigger the making of art – the people's history of art – has still to be told. Georgina Beier's catalytic influence on Kauage is only one recent example of what must have happened very often in the past, in all cultures at all stages of their development. It is just that few people thought to record these crucial occasions. So much art history belittles its subject by tediously searching for similarities, for occasions of influence, instead of concentrating on those occasions when things became different.

George Murray, the naïve artist, played a similar role to Georgina's when he encouraged both his father Josef Szubert and his mother-in-law Margaret Baird to paint. George Murray is exceptional among artists in also being a collector. He has spent a great deal of his life looking for genuine naïve artists, acquiring work from them and getting to know them and their reasons for painting. His photographs of them capture their enthusiasm for life. Art begins here, in their fresh looks. These people, untrained in art, paint only because they want to.

Untrained artists often know, instinctively, that the space in a picture is not like real space – every-

Dora Holzhandler

Wedding Night 1989

OIL ON CANVAS

130 x 103cm

Dora Holzhandler loves painting … 'and being able to express myself, turning my life into art; my thoughts and hopes into beautiful colours and shapes. It's a sort of meditation I suppose, and it makes me happy to see the nature of my own mind.'

thing in it is not dragged down to the bottom by gravity. Things can float about in a picture – just as your eye roves about looking at things from different angles. Dora Holzhandler, though not untrained (page 35), uses this freedom to express the genuine sweetness of newly married love. She is aware of the great paintings of Chagall within her own Jewish tradition, but she laces his free use of space with her own memories to express her more personal delight. Her insistent naïveté is, I think, the way she remains true to her own experience. It is in fact rare for us to look at things from a fixed viewpoint. Usually we move through space, even if only by turning our head from side to side. By doing so, we bring the scene alive and give it three dimensions.

Memories are made up, usually, of different viewpoints of a space we have lived in and walked through. People often want to recall their past and mull it over. Several of the artists George Murray

collected started painting towards the end of their lives. Their pictures are painted from the perspective of memory. In *School Days* (page 34) Margaret Baird has drawn the girls much bigger than the boys – even though the latter are in front. But then the artist was standing with the girls. She also painted the ball (which was quite possibly coming right at them) huge – much bigger than it is now. George and his wife laughed at the size of the ball – not critically, perhaps, but because it was so vivid. Margaret Baird was very upset at their reaction, reduced the size of the ball and did not paint again for months. She was an instinctive artist and had not developed the rationale that would have enabled her to resist the criticism of what she felt was right.

Paul Waplington is by no means a naïve artist even though he never went to an art school. He earned his living as a lace designer, and taught himself to paint. He has developed such drawing

Paul Waplington

View Over Sneinton Dale 1983

OIL ON CANVAS

centre panel 208 x 152cm
wings (each) 175 x 147cm

Nick Waplington

Untitled 1989

PHOTOGRAPHIC PRINT

skills that he can twist and turn the space in his pictures. In View *Over Sneinton Dale* he gives you the sensation that you are one of the kids in his picture, swinging out over the roof-tops. The picture was painted in the mid-1980s, when unemployment was a major issue. It will, I think, come to be seen as a telling image of its time: the kids play, but the question the picture asks is what does the future hold? Politics is brought to life and given personal significance in this magnificent triptych. His art is a remarkable achievement made without the art establishment system – the secure world (once you are in it) of art schools, art dealers and publicly subsidized art galleries.

Nick Waplington, Paul's nephew, has recently earned an international reputation photographing two working-class families in Nottingham. He practically lived with them for a year until they became effectively unaware of his presence. His best photographs capture their lives with a feeling for

rhythm and energy that is celebratory, however uncouth the subject-matter. These insights can be very vivid, but where is Nick Waplington in all this? It is difficult even to know where he is taking the pictures from. The strength of Paul Waplington's painting is that you know where he stands. The anonymity of Nick Waplington's photographs adds to their authenticity, but could also be a limitation.

Beryl Cook never disguises her point of view. She is an example of a painter who has emerged from a naïve beginning, totally untrained, and has developed into an artist of stature and considerable sophistication. She started painting out of irritation with her twelve year old son, who painted pictures with the sky at the top, a house at the bottom and nothing in the middle. He justified himself by saying that there was nothing in the middle. So Beryl painted a picture with something in the middle – a lady with two large breasts. She could not do waists, so she put in a fence, with the breasts hanging over it – hence her car-mechanic husband's title for the picture: *The Hangover*. Beryl told me she was so shocked, physically, by what she had done – she felt as if she had been hit in the stomach – that she did not paint again for two years. When she began again, she painted scenes in her local pub – where she sold her first picture, to her great surprise. Thirty years later, she must now be the most genuinely famous artist working in Britain today.

I invited her up to Glasgow to see if there was anything she would like to paint here which we might acquire for the Gallery of Modern Art. She was a bit hesitant at first because she does not accept commissions. She only paints what she wants to and she could not guarantee she would 'see' anything in Glasgow. She need not have worried. I was with her in the Horseshoe Bar on Karaoke night when I saw her eyes begin to light up, even more than they do usually. She is very good company, but I could see she was becoming more and more interested in the scene around her. Her eyes seemed to dance around the scene, taking everything and everyone in. She opened her handbag and made a few notes on a little pad and occasionally took a flash photo with a little camera. The picture that emerged is not a direct rendition of the scene, but a reinvention of it using elements of the upstairs room at the Horseshoe Bar. Above all, it captures the atmosphere in the place.

Beryl Cook has become one of our best commentators on contemporary life. She does it without cynicism, but with a warmth and humanity that is combined with a sharpness of observation and wit which ensures there is no sentimentality. She paints on a white board with thin glazes of colour so that the light shines through from behind, making the colours glow. The drawing, the defini-tion, is the key to the character and content of each picture. She will spend ages getting an expression just right. It has to be not only right, but in the right place, so that each expression relates to the others to create the lively looks that animate each scene. The expressions of the lady and the dog in *By the Clyde* complement each other in ways I could not possibly explain. This picture began as an observa-tion of a bus going over a bridge. I can never see these orange buses now on a bridge over the Clyde without thinking of Beryl Cook. Paintings change how we see the world. A painter feels what he or she sees and makes us feel it.

By the Clyde is a composite picture. Beryl saw the coat on a lady in Central Station and could not resist using it here. She saw a boulder with the graffiti 'Wogs Out' on it and felt the picture needed that too. Her husband John said she could not possibly put that in because the City Council would not like it. I said it was up to her – she was the artist. Art is not reality; it is like a magical sphere in which the artist can conjure up the reflections of anything they like in the world. Within this sphere, the artist has the freedom of a dictator. Art is a legitimate form of dictatorship within a democracy. Only dictators cannot accept the dictatorship of art. Beryl Cook did put in the graffiti, but faintly – as if the Council had tried but not quite managed to scrub it out.

When it comes to painting graffiti, no one can beat Jock McFadyen. His renderings of it are brilliant displays of virtuosity. Artists are observers of life. McFadyen is drawn to and draws inspiration from the seamier aspects of modern cities. He renders these with the precision and elegance of a whip (page 41). His delicacy of handling and fine sense of colour discover celebratory qualities in scenes that would otherwise be condemned as sordid.

Children are taught that it is rude to stare. A more polite way to look is to let your eyes relax, not look at anything in particular, and take in the whole scene. The Impressionists saw like that. Everything shimmers in their pictures, nothing is solid. Artists like McFadyen and Cook cannot stop themselves staring. Everything they concentrate on becomes sharp and clear. Objects in McFadyen's sights become painful; in Cook's they become edible. Her eye draws things closer to her, as if she is hungry for them. Everything she draws, from a cigarette butt up, becomes monumental, expressing as it does her appetite for life. She is the most recent manifesta-tion of that rich seam in British art that goes back through Edward Burra and the saucy postcards of Donald McGill to the Music Hall and beyond.

Art springs from life, not from art. Artists are often very interested in other artists' work – but they pick and choose who interests them for their own special reasons. John Byrne is such a brilliant draughtsman and painter – he was trained at the Glasgow School of Art – that he can produce almost any style at will. Out of wickedness, perhaps, but partly, I believe, because he wanted to widen his vocabulary and scope as an artist, he invented

another persona for himself – the naïve painter 'Patrick' (named after his father). He achieved considerable success at this, and saw no reason, until very recently, to kill the impostor off. Some of his most haunting pictures such as *The American Boy* (page 42) and famous works (like his portrait of The Beatles) were produced in this *faux naïve* style, and reached an audience that would probably have eluded him if he had done as he ought. Disregarding any fear of being dismissed as 'literary' – the unforgivable sin as far as an artist in the sixties and seventies was concerned – he wrote plays and film scripts. *Tutti Frutti*, his account of the life of an ageing rock band, is a classic of modern television.

Beryl Cook
Karaoke 1992
OIL ON BOARD
82 x 89cm

B.Cook

Beryl Cook

By the Clyde 1992

OIL ON BOARD

88 x 60cm

Beryl Cook's choice of subject is often triggered by
personal experience – 'I know people are cheered by
the paintings, and I like to think I'm giving back some
of the pleasure I've always had in the activities going
on around me.'

Jock McFadyen

Depression 1990

OIL ON CANVAS

198 x 198cm

John Byrne
The American Boy 1971
OIL ON BOARD (TWO PANELS)
213 x 244cm

All this and an artist too – but why not? Some day, perhaps, all these personae will come together.

One of the key things an artist has to do is to develop a style that is expressive of his or her personality, yet at the same time is capable of saying what he or she wants to say. To be personal and profound is one of the key challenges for artists today. Some artists have gone so far as to make art out of their everyday lives. Bruce Lacey's *Head*, which is being specially made for our gallery and cannot be illustrated at the time of writing, invites you in one ear and out the other. In between you sit in the palm of his hand and see his life's art roll past on video screens. Lacey was one of the first to make robotic art. He also made assemblages out of rubbish (*Schooldays* shows what he feels we do to

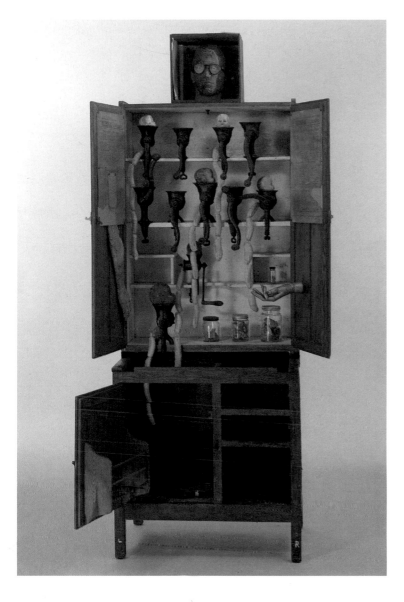

Bruce Lacey
Schooldays 1963
WOOD, METAL, PLASTIC, CLOTH, RUBBER
222 x 140 x 79cm

kids), and did performance art. Once when he was invited to speak at a seminar on art and censorship, he went wearing a long raincoat but said nothing. When asked to speak, he just stood up and opened his coat – his trousers began at his knees, his shirt stopped at his chest and – *pace* Beryl – there was nothing in the middle. He is one of the most creative people in British post-war art. Many artists have been influenced by him but he has no 'school'. He has made an artistic statement of his life, saying: be yourself.

Many artists I have met are most interested in talking about themselves. This is not necessarily, or simply egotism; it is often just that nothing interests them more than what they are doing next. They can be as wide-ranging and responsive as anyone, but in the end they are always searching for anything that can feed their creativity. That is the job our society gives artists: to be themselves. Jo Spence developed a distinct language to do this – photography with commentary. She cast herself as herself in the play of her life. Her art accumulated like a monumental scrap-book of her own performances. Her set pieces began wittily, with many references to the role of women in society. As cancer took a grip on her, she became more absorbed with her inner feelings, though without losing her political edge, as for example in *Narratives of Dis-Ease* (page 44). She even planned how she wanted to be photographed after her death. I know of nothing like it in the history of art.

The next millennium will in my opinion be the

Jo Spence

Included? from *Narratives of Dis-Ease:
Ritualized Procedures* 1990

PHOTOGRAPHIC PRINT

91 x 61cm

'In displaying this work (as I displayed my body previously for each of the medical, the familial, the media and the male gazes) I am aware that these images can shock. Breaking out is not a painless process for me. In cracking the mirror for myself I cannot help but challenge your view too. Nor are these offered as great artworks, but to stimulate you into thinking how you could represent the fantasy of your everyday life.'

Jo Spence
Return to Nature 1991–2
PHOTOGRAPHIC PRINT
91 x 61cm

age of women. Evidence of this can, I think, be seen in the growing number of significant women artists. In my opinion, one of the finest living artists in the world today is Niki de Saint-Phalle. She began, too, by making art of her life. She was born into high society, half-French, half-American. She worked first as a model and appeared on the cover of *Time* magazine in 1949 as a glamorous debutante. In 1955 she suffered a severe mental breakdown, and since painting had helped her recover, she decided to give up her ideas of becoming an actress to concentrate on art. Her early pictures are naïve in style, showing palaces and gardens with fantastic beasts in them – eventually she made these real as sculptures in her magical *Tarot Garden* in Italy (page 65).

At first she lived her art. She made assemblages of objects and covered these with plaster – burying with them sacks of wet paint. Then, when the plaster had dried, standing at some distance, aiming her .22 rifle, she shot her own work till all the sacks of paint buried under the plaster had burst and bled (see *Autel du Chat Mort* page 46).

She was destroying, with great satisfaction, her previous life, and all its indicators of success – social, religious, economic and personal. In time, these images of destruction gave way to images of creation – huge, playful female figures, brightly coloured, leaping for joy, hymns to love. Since the late 1960s, her sculptures, paintings and drawings have always had joy in them, even if they deal with evil. Niki de Saint-Phalle has developed a visual language that is at once personal, that is recognizably hers, and at the same time capable of encom-

passing the big experiences of our lives, both love and death. The opposite of fear of death is love of life, as Cyril Connolly observed, and one of the great challenges for artists today is to be positive without being sentimental – to be hopeful without shielding themselves at all from suffering. Art must be positive, otherwise there would be no point in making it. That is why this gallery places such an emphasis on creating art rather than just perceiving it.

David Hockney, whose work will feature in a major way in the gallery once his huge exhibition project with us is complete, shows an ever increasing grip on the joy-creating capacity of art. If the kids in Paul Waplington's painting (pages 36–37) swing out over the roof tops so that the whole landscape rocks, Hockney takes us on a flight which is not a flight of fancy or fantasy but a journey of discovery into real experience. As with Bridget Riley's paintings (pages 22, 62), the experience of looking at one of Hockney's recent paintings leaves you in wonderment that seeing can itself be so exhilarating. He told me his sister had once said to him when she was a kid that she thought space was God. Walking around Glasgow, or anywhere, with David Hockney makes you much more aware of your visual environment. He pointed out to me, for example, how beautifully the streets are proportioned in the Blythswood Square area, how the height of the buildings related to balancing the width of each street. His art is grounded in reality; it is sensuous and intellectual; it has guts.

One reason why Picasso's output was so huge is because he found so much joy in making things. He

Niki de Saint-Phalle
Autel du Chat Mort 1962

MIXED MEDIA

286 x 250 x 79cm

The artist has written: 'The painting was the victim. WHO was the painting? Daddy? All Men? Small Men? Tall Men? Big Men? Fat Men? Men? My brother John? Or was the painting ME: Did I shoot at myself during a RITUAL which enabled me to die by my own hand and be reborn? I was immortal!…

'I was shooting at MYSELF, society with its injustices. I was shooting at my own violence and the violence of the times. By shooting at my own violence, I no longer had to carry it inside me like a burden.'

made a very elegant, prehistoric bull's head out of a bicycle saddle and a pair of handlebars. Since then, many artists have put together objects they have found to create something new. Ron O'Donnell builds whole sets in his garage out of all the stuff he collects, and then photographs them to create his funny, acerbic images of our foibles and more harmful fantasies. David Kemp (page 48) supposes himself to be an archaeologist years in the future discovering relics of our own culture. He then puts these together in the way he imagines they were used by us, not in a functional way because their functions have long been lost, but as votive figures. Thus he creates images of the real gods and goddesses that govern our age. His sculptures are strong, funny and highly inventive. He does not cheat, by altering something to make it fit or look better. Tragically he recently lost most of his pantheon of the *Tribe That Held The Sky Up* in a fire, and our collection contains some of the few of his relics of our age to survive.

Eduard Bersudsky learned his skills as a wood-carver making traditional figures for children's play-grounds in and around St Petersburg (then Leningrad). One day he made one of his carved figures move. He was so surprised by what he saw

Ron O'Donnell

The Scotsman 1987

PHOTOGRAPHIC PRINT

183 x 274cm

'When looking at the image afterwards, he felt the shock of recognition: "I suddenly realised it was me. That's where I used to be with a pencil in my hand, copying The Beano and The Dandy."'

Quotation taken with kind permission from an interview between the artist and Sally Kinnes, *Scotland on Sunday* 17 May 1992.

David Kemp

Iron Horse: equestrian cult figure
Dept. of Antiquities G07 636 083
WELDED STEEL
189 x 142 x 69cm

The Tribe that held the sky up, shown at the McLellan Galleries in 1991, was in effect a fake museum of objects supposedly excavated then pieced together. A scrap of paper accompanied the fictitious hoard, bearing the following legend:
'There once was a clever tribe.

Their knowledge tied the four corners of the world together.
Their sorcerers had many powers.
They made great poles that held the sky up.
They had great cunning with fire.
They made the night like day.
They could send pictures in the wind.
Their long tongues could speak over many miles.

Their warriors were fierce and powerful.
They rose in the air, over land and sea.
They overcame all the other tribes of the earth.

One day, the smoke from their many clevernesses grew thick.
Great fires sprang up.
The flames licked up the poles and burned a hole in the sky.
Slowly the sky started to fall.

The tribe feared the dreadful weight of the clouds.
They dug deep holes in the earth.
There they hid with all their clever things.
Here they wait, until the day the sky is pushed back up.'

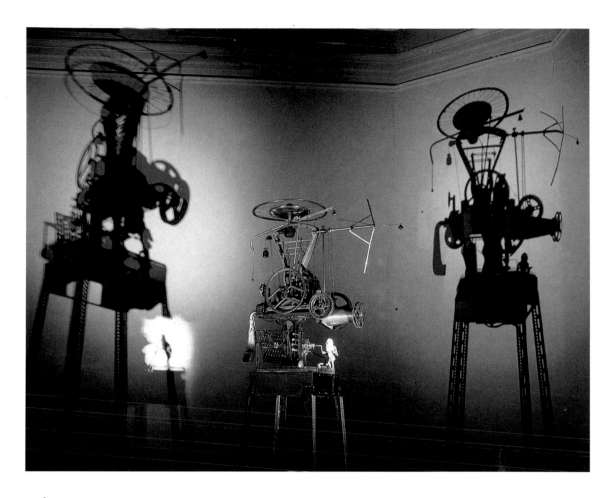

that he told me that he leapt back a yard. In the same way, Beryl Cook felt as if she had been punched in the stomach when she painted her first picture, so surprised was she by the result. Once he began to make moving figures, Bersudsky could not stop. He used bits of wood thrown away by others to create elaborate machines and towers, peopled with figures – all of them pulling each others' strings. These expressed his views on Communism and the people who ran it – the tragedy and comedy of life under the system.

Several of his friends were disappearing into Siberia, and he became so depressed that he became an elective mute. Only his art spoke. The authorities considered his art just 'toys', so this truly dissident artist survived. His work was discovered by Tatiana Jakovskaia, who was then working in the theatre. She realized that it would be possible to present these sculptures to the public as a performance – so the Sharmanka Theatre was born, with all its sound effects and lighting. Tatiana realized that no-one would come at first, because who had ever heard of a theatre of sculptures? So she invited

Eduard Bersudsky
The Great Idea (Karl Marx)
MIXED MEDIA CONSTRUCTION
267 x 118 x 62cm

a leading company of mime artists to perform among them, each gradually freezing as the sculptures came to life. The performance was symbolic of Bersudsky's own personal recovery. Not only did people begin to see his sculptures, but his work began to gain in confidence and scale – and gradually the artist himself began to speak again.

Influenced by an exhibition he saw of the Swiss kinetic artist Jean Tinguely's work, Bersudsky began to use metal and other scrap in his work. *The Great Idea (Karl Marx)* (page 49) is one of the funniest and saddest commentaries on Communism I have ever seen. The little wooden figure of Karl Marx begins by turning the handle. Slowly the whole contraption above him – made out of bits of machinery that Russians would instantly recognize as the products of Soviet factories – begins to spring to life. As he turns the handle faster, the whole ensemble begins to rotate, swinging bits of itself around in a mad dance, while a chorus of workers can be heard

singing: 'Our train will fly. We will not be stopped because we have bayonets in our hands.' But then the machine and the soundtrack start to falter and grind to a halt. Still Marx goes on turning the handle, but nothing else is moving. Everything has seized up and the only sound to be heard is one of birds singing. The whole tale takes about five minutes.

It would be impossible to describe here all that happens in the machine Bersudsky made to express his feelings about Perestroika (complete political reorganisation), except to say that sequences of ominousness and playfulness, hope and fear finally get consumed in chaos. Something of the same feelings is expressed in *Psychedelic Attack of the Blue Rabbits* by Oleg Holosiy (opposite) which is based on the painting *In the Line of Fire* (1916) by Petrov Vodkin. This showed Tsarist soldiers defending Russia, some are shooting, others are being killed. By quoting this famous picture, Holosiy

Eduard Bersudsky

An Autumn Walk in the Era of Perestroika
'Meta-Tinguely'
MIXED MEDIA CONSTRUCTION
307 x 381 x 122cm

'It tells the story of Gorbachev's Perestroika, ushered in
by the station break of Radio Moscow, from 1917
onwards pretending to be the signal of a new era for
the whole of the world. Alas, like the great idea of Karl
Marx, the Perestroika is soon hampered by its own
mechanisms and thus incapable to escape failure and
deformation. Thus the symbols of progress, the horse
and the shoes, don't get off the mark, but instead the
gun-barrel starts moving and people fall prey to all
kinds of vulgarities.'

Oleg Holosiy

Psychedelic Attack of the Blue Rabbits 1990
OIL ON CANVAS
200 x 300cm

Steven Campbell
Painting in Defence of Migrants 1993
OIL ON CANVAS
272 x 257cm

suggested the possibility that the good intentions of Perestroika could result in nationalism, dictatorship and war. Holosiy died tragically in 1993. Bersudsky has now moved his theatre out of Russia and has settled in Glasgow.

Bersudsky discovers his sculptures as he makes them. He has an idea in his head when he starts, but this changes and develops as he works on it. It is the same for all creative artists. They do not illustrate what they know but discover new things as they work. Steven Campbell knew this when he was a student at Glasgow School of Art. He was there at an interesting time, with Currie, Wiszniewski and Howson. He exerted a powerful influence partly because of his determination to be an artist – he was older than the rest having spent seven years as a steel fitter – and he wrote later 'I didn't go to Art School to train to be a teacher.' Campbell knew that you do things by doing them. He developed a way of painting, a personal vocabulary of images, that enabled him to invent as he painted. About *Painting in Defence of Migrants* (opposite) he wrote:

> This picture is a comment on how people are vulnerable. All the birds are migrants. Although we are cruel to nature and there are hunters in the sky and clouds, I wanted to convey the idea that when people are in terrible circumstances, nature still has a sensitivity. Because we are part of nature, it will come to our defence when things are so bad. The people are migrants and they are exhausted, but the migrant birds help them. I think it is a defence of sensitivity.

Adrian Wiszniewski (Campbell's fellow student in Glasgow) is also an artist of invention – I was going to write 'poet' because his distinct voice was clear almost from the first. *Weeds in a Landscape* is a superb expression of this 'voice'. If you look closely at the canvas, you will see how each line seems to grow as an echo of its neighbour, unfolding or folding, leaving or loving, caressing or flowering. Everywhere you look there is growing invention – as if the artist had breathed across the canvas and it has rippled into life. Wiszniewski probably would not like this description – he would prefer to call the ripples 'squiggles,' just as he has called the flowers of youth in the picture 'weeds'; but he would not deny that the joy was for him in the painting – and we can relive that by watching his imagination grow on the canvas.

Adrian Wiszniewski

Weeds in a Landscape 1989

OIL ON CANVAS

346 x 213cm

'I always make my figures in such a way that you can't tell the difference between somebody who's left wing or right wing, good or bad. You can't judge political convictions or morals from people's faces.'

John Bellany
The Fishers 1966
OIL ON HARDBOARD
182 x 213cm

John Bellany
Journey to the End of the Night 1972
OIL ON CANVAS

left panel   209 x 139cm
centre panel 210 x 181cm
right panel   209 x 138cm

John Bellany never misses a moment, if he can help it, away from 'the brushes' He knows that only by painting will anything happen, will anything be achieved. He is one of those naturally gifted artists for whom painting and drawing were natural forms of expression. He knew he could communicate with others through them – and not only to others, but also with himself. That is why painting for him is such a joyful activity – doing it, he discovers more and more. Artistic creation is like a conversation with yourself (and sometimes with others). Some people take to particular languages, like music or words or painting, from a very early age and find when they practise them all sorts of delights are revealed.

John Bellany's life is laid out in his studio: his upbringing in the little fishing ports on the east coast of Scotland – intimate, passionate communities of poor, hard-working people, riven through with extreme puritan views about sex and drink and song, hard pressed against the perilous backdrop of the sea. Danger provides the background for Bellany's joy. Whether he is exploring his feelings after a visit to the Buchenwald Concentration Camp in 1967, or living (and painting his way) through a liver transplant operation, at his own death's door in 1988 (page 72), his paint is always sensitive, his drawing delicate and his colour strong.

Bellany's painting is robust enough to carry even the most disturbing visions, such as *Journey to the End of the Night* (opposite and below). This is a nightmare in yellow and black. We have left the sea and are in a cave – a cross between a bedroom and a chapel, in which strange sexual and primitive rites are being carried out. The painting takes its form from a medieval altarpiece; these usually show a major scene from the Christian story, such the Madonna and Child or the Crucifixion in the centre, flanked on either side by portraits of saints carrying the symbols of their martyrdom. Like Niki de Saint-Phalle's *Autel du Chat Mort* (page 46), the painting seems to be a cry of pain against oppressive belief. The yellow is the intensity of suffering rather than the light of hope; its glow contrasts with the blacks that bar and brace and bind everything.

Religion is deeply ingrained in Scottish culture

Alexander Guy
Crib VII 1992
OIL ON CANVAS
173 x 203cm

Craigie Aitchison
Crucifixion VII 1988–9
OIL ON CANVAS
213 x 178cm

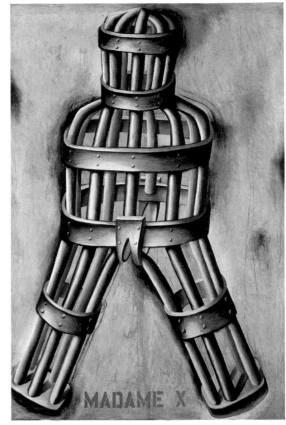

Alexander Guy
Crucifixion 1992
OIL ON CANVAS
208 x 175cm

In 1992 Guy visited Graceland, the former home of Elvis Presley, and became fascinated with the Elvis myth. During work on a series of Elvis paintings he made a few notes:

'August 1992: Jesus died for our sins, Elvis died for our 20th century sins. If Jesus is alive today then so is Elvis. The fact is they are both dead and alive so Jesus = Elvis.

'November 1992: The Elvis suit is not Elvis. It is the myth. It is astronauts, Klu Klux clan, Military, God, Rock n' Roll, Burden, Self-protection, Martyrdom, TV Evangelism, Cult, Fashion and Shroud.'

Alexander Guy
Madame XII 1992–3
OIL ON CANVAS
264 x 173cm

Guy once attended a wedding at which the approving guests were shown a blood-stained sheet to prove the bride's virginity. The words the artist wrote at the time find echoes in *Madame XII*.

'November 1992: If Mary had slept with Joseph and lost her virginity, instead of a night of passion with God, then life would have been a lot simpler for everyone, especially women, over the last 2000 years – sex, guilt, pornography, religion.'

Peter Angermann

Baggersee 1988

OIL ON CANVAS

170 x 220cm

and surfaces in the work of Craigie Aitchison (page 56), and the passionate religious imagery of a young artist like Sandy Guy. His pictures, *Crucifixion* (page 57), *Madame XII* (page 57) and *Crib* (page 56) were not painted as a triptych, but when I suggested we should hang them as such, the artist agreed. They are not about a specific religion but they are about obsessive ideas that can cripple our nature. *Crib* is a variant, in a way, on the theme of Bruce Lacey's *Schooldays* (page 43), only here the child has even less chance because the torture begins earlier.

The artist's job is to see clearly. Paint enables Guy to brush in his vision with bold, strong strokes and vivid lights and darks. He does not tidy up the edges, but once it is there leaves it dripping fresh and naked. Peter Angermann does the same; his images (above) though freely sketched in, are as clear as a bell. As is his colour. Both Guy and Angermann use their incisive visual wit (black

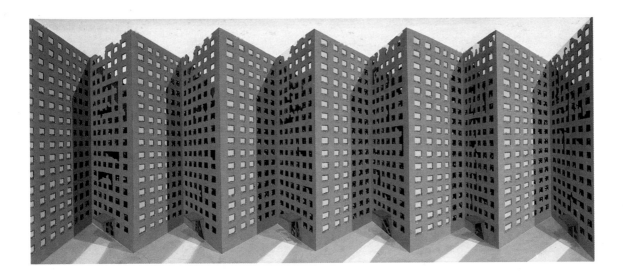

skeletons!) to comment on the world. They do not do this literally but poetically. It is difficult to say exactly what *Baggersee* (opposite) means. It is based on an artificial lake near Nuremberg where Angermann used to swim. He begins a painting in his studio with a very general idea. Only as he works on it do the elements in it emerge until it looks complete – as if he has seen it as a whole. His pictures look as though they are painted quickly all in one go, but in fact they can take days or months. He spends a lot of time thinking, but he works fast when he knows what he wants to put in.

Both Sandy Guy and Peter Angerman's paintings appear bright. They use tone (contrasts of white and black) and hue (in Angerman's case vibrant contrasts of colour) to create a lively sensation in the eye of the onlooker. This sensation can be called the 'light' of a picture. This is a very elusive quality that happens in the mind of the viewer rather than in the picture and is very difficult to write about because it involves the science and psychology of perception. Patrick Hughes' picture (above) physically projects as a low relief, but one sees it as receding and as a result the space within the picture seems to glow more brightly.

This light can be very subtle as in the collages of Francis Davison (page 60), or very forthcoming, as in the paintings of Bridget Riley (pages 22, 62). Davison was one of the most retiring artists I have ever met; he did not sign, title or date his work, and was reluctant to say anything at all about it. It was a visual experience you were either interested in or not. What more was there to say? He worked in the front room of his house, with a white blind drawn

Patrick Hughes
The Shadow of War 1993
OIL ON BOARD
85 x 189 x 17cm

'This picture was prompted by making a film about the war in Bosnia. My pieces are both made in perspective and made the wrong way around. They are planes which fit together in a rectangle to describe space.

'Shadows are helpful allies which differentiate those planes they darken from the ones in the light.

'The parts of the buildings – akin to Sarajevo's tower blocks – in the shadow are being destroyed by shelling. Those in the glow of the sun are radiant and have flowering window boxes.

'I studied to be a teacher rather than an artist, although I had a show in London the day I ended my studies. Perhaps there is a didactic element in my work. But I hope to let people experience *The Shadow of War*, rather than hector them about it. My work does move and the movement is provided by you.'

Francis Davison

Scarlet and Rose in Deep Sea Blue c.1970

COLLAGE

120 x 120cm

down over the window so that the light was muted. A grey day is best for his colours. All he did was to build up abstract compositions with pieces of torn or cut coloured paper. He never painted these colours but used the paper as it came, straight from the factory. He was only interested in how he could make the colours he had been given glow and change, one against another, and how he could make them move in space.

As he learned more and more how to do this, his collages became bigger and freer and bigger still. To many visitors to the gallery, Davison's collages will probably look at first glance the least interesting things on display – and when I first saw them I too found the crumpled and torn edges difficult to accept. But when you take time to respond to the colours and shapes and movements, you discover a superb artist, like an illuminator of a Celtic manu-script living half-hidden in retreat today. These pictures glow with their own quite extraordinary inner light.

Francis Davison was married to the Scottish artist Margaret Mellis, who gave the gallery this collection of his work. Mellis never doubted she was an artist, or doubted what that was. She has referred to herself as being 'like glass' and when you meet her you know what this means: she has a directness of looking that is not modified in any way – her look feels almost physically tangible. She now works with driftwood and scrapwood, relating each piece to each other until they come together as complete images in her mind.

Bridget Riley discovered early that, for her, the important light in a picture was not that which was within, but what was in front of it. You have to stand at a certain distance in front of a painting by Bridget Riley and let your eyes relax to take in the whole picture before you begin to get the whole effect. What you will then see will be quite amazing and totally unreproducible in a book. Her art has to be experienced, not just seen. What happens is that, as you look, the colours (including black and white) trigger off the sensing devices inside your eye in a way that makes the picture appear to dance, move, vibrate, and change colour before your eyes. This activity can be gentle as in *Arrest III* (page 22) or what I can only describe as sonorous, rising to a glorious crescendo as in *Punjab* (page 62). Once you have enjoyed this, you are not likely ever to forget the experience.

Bridget Riley's studio, which takes up the whole of a large terrace house in London, is painted entirely white – the floor, walls and ceilings, even the furniture. By day, light pours in from the large windows at the front and back, while at night carefully balanced fluorescent tubes make the house blaze with an approximation of daylight. Entering it at any time is like moving into a well of light. The only colours in the place are those she is working on in her paintings. Nothing could contrast more with Ken Currie's dark, cavernous studio, with boards over the windows to mask off all natural light, the walls hung with sketches, photographs and reproductions of things he is interested in at the time, the whole interior lit only to the level he needs to work by.

Most modern art galleries provide a uniformity of setting for their collection, with the good intentions of creating an anonymous environment in

Margaret Mellis
Pandora's Red Box 1992
CONSTRUCTION
25 x 34 x 36cm

'I spent a horrible lonely evening in an empty flat with nothing to eat. The party was next door. I had been excluded, although I knew the hostess well.

'Next morning, going to the train I saw a curious red box lying in the middle of the road, lid in the air. I immediately imagined filling it with bright colours which would jam the door so that it could never shut again.

'I put the box in the studio. Red is a lovely colour, it harmonizes all other colours and eats the dirt (transforms dirt into tone). Suddenly pieces of painted wood came out of my wood pile and went into the box like a swarm of bees. The door was jammed open for ever. When everything stopped happening I thought of Pandora. This was another version of Pandora's box.'

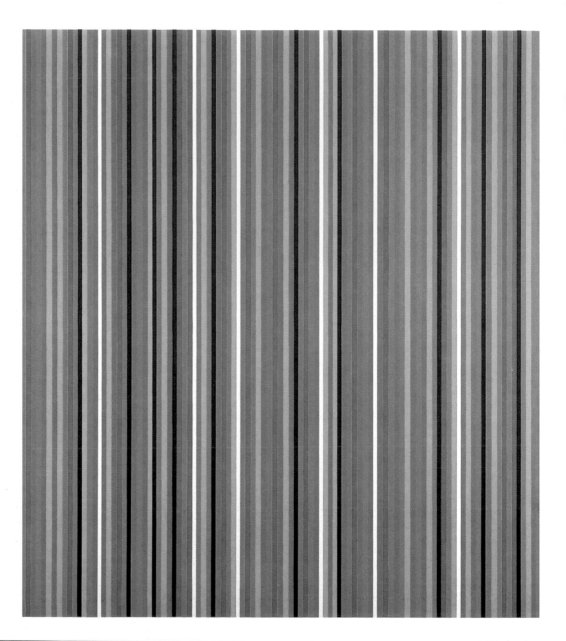

Bridget Riley
Luxor 1982
OIL ON LINEN
224 x 198cm

Bridget Riley
Punjab 1971
ACRYLIC ON CANVAS
145 x 365cm

'The tautness of the horizontal bands firmly establishes the structure over which our eyes can play, very much as though they were the bow being drawn across the strings of a musical instrument, giving rise to sensation. In *Punjab* the movement rises, through big, slow soft reds, reaching its greatest intensity towards the top of the canvas, where little fast, sharp reds take over and, interspersed with greens, blues and whites, hint at mellow warmth, violet cools and bright, bright light.'

Hex
Generator 1966
COMPUTER GENERATED IMAGE

which to show off the individuality of each piece. What tends to happen, however, is that while one work of art will benefit from this, another will suffer. The visitors, particularly those who are not used to modern art galleries, can be left with the feeling that the setting is more important than the art. In our Gallery of Modern Art we have taken a different view. Firstly, the visitor's individual experience of each work of art is considered to be more important than the overall effect. The art and the visitor will, we hope, be more important than the architecture and the curator! Secondly, we have taken advantage of the very varied spaces in the building to create different emotional environments for the works on show. A painting by Bridget Riley and one by Ken Currie should not be hung in the same environment because they were not created in the same environment. It is a falsification of their art to put them together in this way. Our Gallery of Modern Art emphasizes difference and by doing so proposes that modern art is not a continuum validated by a curator, but a kaleidoscope of different insights into the nature of our existence.

To emphasize the different atmospheres we want to create on each floor, we have called the different galleries after the elements that Aristotle believed to be the basis of everything: Air, Fire, Earth and Water. We put Fire in the basement, and made it the centre for creativity in action – particularly those artists such as Hex (below) who are exploring

the extraordinary possibilities that modern technology opens up for image-making and communication. At the ground level is the Earth Gallery with its arcades of stone pillars, suitable for showing large scale painting and sculpture. On the first floor are the Water galleries, with the long, running spaces and side lighting suitable for showing drawing and photography and more narrative art. At the top, we put Air. We have done our best there to create a sensation of light everywhere, falling from the roof and reflected up from the floor. We want no shadows here, no barriers, no drama, just an ambient light, as if one were walking on air. That is the atmosphere of Bridget Riley's studio. It is also the sensation of the white canvas on the easel.

Some artists begin by looking at the world, then concentrate on what interests them by leaving things out. Others begin with nothing – an empty canvas – and build up a picture from there. This is like the difference between a Shakespearian tragedy and a Japanese Noh drama. Shakespeare begins with the noise of the world and leads you to a moment of silence and death. Japanese Noh drama begins with silence and stillness and slowly builds up to a dance. John McLean (opposite) adopts the Eastern approach. His art relies on making the right mark on nothing. This requires concentration, thought, feeling and daring, so that everything he wants to say can be contained in the one action. When you tune your mind to McLean's art, the colour and shapes in his paintings dance. The title *Strathspey* may not conjure up for you an image of people dancing, but McLean's picture is actually closer than a representational painting would have been to conveying the sensation of the dance itself.

Many Eastern philosophies share a belief in the oneness of everything. They tend to see negative and positive forces (or evil and good in our terms) not as opposites fighting each other for dominion, but as two sides of one coin, both essential to each other. In the same way, body and soul are not seen as divided, but as part of each other. Physical action equates to 'spiritual' action, so a painting can track the activity of the 'soul'. Many Western artists, like Alan Davie (page 66), have been influenced by such Eastern philosophies. Each painting for him is a journey of discovery into a joyous linear world of colour, light and movement, of memory and energy and imagination, of feelings and thoughts slowly

John McLean
Strathspey 1993
ACRYLIC ON CANVAS
225 x 158cm

'My works have no hidden meaning. To understand, all you have to do is look. Everything only works in relation to everything else in the painting… Looking triggers imagination and association.

'I only work in terms of the feelings I can elicit with drawing, colour and surface… Instinct and spontaneity are crucial. Thought goes into it too, in the same way it does in singing and dancing.'

Alan Davie working on the *Magician* for Niki de Saint-Phalle's *Tarot Garden* at Garavicchio in Tuscany

Alan Davie
Cornucopia 1960
OIL ON CANVAS
213 x 173cm

surfacing or tumbling out thick and fast as in his *Cornucopia* (opposite) of delight. Davie loved diving in the seas of St Lucia (where he used to live every winter), or gliding above the hills of England (where he spent the summers) and journeying to fascinating places around the world, like Australia and South America. In just the same way, he loves diving and gliding and journeying through his mind, by means of his art. This is why Niki de Saint-Phalle invited him to paint the inside of the head on the figure of the *Magician* (page 65) in her *Tarot Garden*. In her Tarot pack the Magician is card number one. His words for her are 'Creation. Work is a Game. Concentration without Effort. Action'.

Hock-Aun Teh is one of the first Eastern artists, to my knowledge, to use Western abstract painting methods to express his own native philosophy. He was born in Malaysia and studied traditional painting in the Chinese manner. He then came to Glasgow School of Art to learn Western techniques and he has remained here ever since, returning regularly to Malaysia to steep himself in his native culture, and visit the jungle. He is a master of martial arts, specializing in tae kwon do and tukido. For him, physical energy (page 68), is no different from artistic energy. Both activities are natural and, he feels, essential to his well-being. He says of exercise, and of painting, that 'true enjoyment comes from within'.

Recently Hock-Aun Teh's art has become richer. He has begun to develop a visual language that enables him to tell stories. Though we are used to abstract signs and symbols all around us – the letters you are reading now are one example – many people still find it difficult to accept abstraction in art. The Chinese do not have this difficulty partly because their written language itself is pictorial. The Chinese word for a house is based on a simplified drawing of a house. This means that Chinese painting and writing are extensions of each other. A Chinese painting contains all sorts of punning meanings that are totally lost on people who cannot read Chinese. We can make an art of writing (the most beautiful I know at present is the letter cutting of Lida Lopes Cardozo and her late husband David Kindersley), or you can make images with words, as the Scottish concrete poet, installation artist and gardener, Ian Hamilton Finlay. But for the Chinese, art and writing are one. This is why Hock-Aun Teh

Ian Hamilton Finlay
Star/Steer 1966
SCREENPRINT
57 x 45cm

Hock-Aun Teh
Fitness is Energy 1987
ACRYLIC ON CANVAS
183 x 153cm

Hock-Aun Teh
The Milky Way – A Chinese myth
ACRYLIC ON PAPER
155 x 150cm

has been able to develop his art of abstract story telling.

The Milky Way – A Chinese myth (above) captures the moment when the Empress of Heaven took a hairpin out of her hair and angrily tore it across the heavens to make the Milky Way. She did this to create a river of light that would separate her daughter from the man who was trying to take her back to earth to be his wife. The painting does not illustrate the story any more than John McLean's

illustrates a Scottish dance. These paintings communicate experience more directly than that.

W H Auden defined poetry as 'memorable speech'. We do not have a word for speaking to each other visually. Perhaps the nearest equivalent definition for art would be that it is a memorable visual experience. One of the signs of a good painting is that the experience of looking at it stays with you for a long time afterwards. The best art is unforgettable.

Money and Art

Sir William Burrell correctly anticipated this century's two World Wars. Before both of them he bought ships cheaply which he sold later at peak prices. The money he made he turned into art, which he gave to the city for its lasting good. Many now try to turn art into money. By predicting an artist's fame, they hope that they can buy cheap today what they can sell dear tomorrow. Certainly by the seventeenth century, art, both modern and old, had come to be valued as an investment. It is as an investment that modern art is primarily valued today. I should perhaps say 'priced', not 'valued', because you cannot put a price on artistic value; you cannot really sell an artistic experience, any more than you can sell a lover's kiss.

The trouble is that art comes in a unique casement that can itself be bought and sold, even if the experience gained from looking at it cannot. It is as if there was only one example of Beethoven's Ninth Symphony – on one record. Think how valuable that would be! Music is re-creatable (and now reproducible) in a way that art is not. You pay the same price for a score (or a disc) no matter how good or bad the music is. There is no equivalent equitable distribution for art, except through public art galleries. That is why they are so important. Just because art is unique, because it is hand-made, does not invalidate it in our modern world (rather the reverse, as I have tried to prove), but it does make it essential that we get the distribution system right. What better case can there be for public ownership – for the existence and proliferation of public art galleries?

There can come a point in the history of a work of art when it ceases to be an individual's property and comes to belong quite naturally to everyone. In this way the art of the past becomes our heritage and enters our museums with some degree of consensus. There is, however, no such consensus about modern art entering public ownership, nor can there be. It is too soon for it to have been sifted through time and for its lasting qualities to have emerged. That is why some people feel that modern art should not be in museums at all, but in the streets. I would have a lot of sympathy with this view if every street were an art gallery! Until such time as they are, we need galleries to show art, because art is one of the vital means by which we communicate with each other. Our lives are the poorer if society provides no outlet for this form of expression. I have tried in this introduction to show how natural the making of art can be, and how some people just cannot stop themselves doing it, no matter how many obstacles are put in their way!

The illustration shows Arthur Wright painting in his greenhouse because his wife said his work made a mess in the house.

The only criterion for modern art entering a public art gallery is its quality. This has, in the end, to be a question of personal judgement based on experience. Some art, like Beryl Cook's, is validated in the public domain, by the huge sales of reproductions of her work. Some originals of her work, which enable its full quality to be enjoyed, should, therefore, be in public galleries. Most artists never get a chance to reach a wider public except through the gallery system.

This puts a great responsibility on the selectors of the art seen in our public galleries. They have to exercise judgement much like commissioning editors for a publisher or TV company – they have to know their art and their audience and have the insight to respond to what is new.

Unlike galleries showing historical art, modern art galleries, therefore, have to be leaders rather than followers in their sphere. Of course they are dependent on the artists as they are dependent on the public, but they are not dependent on any other filter of judgement. I am advocating here an actively positive, rather than a discretely passive, role for modern art galleries within society.

Lord Gowrie, Conservative Minister for the Arts (1981–3), and a chairman of Sotheby's from 1985, suggested to me that curators in modern art galleries could not do better than follow the dealers. I can understand his belief in this, for art dealers have at least to test the art they sell in the market place and that in itself is some form of validation. However markets can be created as every advertising agency knows, and products can certainly be hyped to make them appear exclusive. Many dealers are clever at marketing and restrict the number of artists they show to make what they have even more exclusive. Their aim is to get their artists on to the bottom rung of the investment ladder. Once there, the artist's work should go on increasing in value over the years. Public galleries can play a key role in providing this crucial leg-up; an acquisition by them can be an indication that an artist's work is of historical value and as a result his or her prices go up. Galleries, therefore, play a role in the art market and they can, if they are not careful, find themselves being led by it rather than providing a healthy alternative.

I learned my lesson about the artificiality of the art market years ago when I was at an art auction. A record price was paid for one of the lots. To my surprise, the room broke into applause and many went to congratulate the buyer. I naïvely thought people should have commiserated with him for having had to pay so much. But then I realized that by managing to pay so much, the buyer had raised the value of the other dealers' current stock. No wonder they were all pleased!

Public art galleries should not be interested in money because they are not acquiring work to resell. They need only be interested in the artistic value of each piece. A high price, like a gold frame, is not a guarantee of quality. Combined with the very considerable pressure of the art middle men both in the public and private spheres, this can make it difficult at times not to begin to doubt your own responses. We have been helped here by not having too attractive a budget. We have approximately £250,000 a year to spend on art. That may seem a lot, but when you consider it buys half a Hockney, or a quarter of a Francis Bacon, it is not that much. In comparison also with other galleries of modern art, we are rather small fry: Scotland's National Gallery of Modern Art (based in Edinburgh) was spending over twice this sum every year as long ago as the 1970s. So we have had to be more inventive in what we buy and how we work with artists and their dealers.

We have attempted to go back to the sources of contemporary creativity. Art cannot be made just to make money. If it were, no one would buy it – unless, as happens too often today, people think they can make money themselves by doing so! In beginning this collection, we have looked for the unadulterated springs of creativity. As a public gallery, we have been able to look at art neither as an investment nor as a milestone in some spurious history but as an experience for people to enjoy. We can only hope that our enjoyment is shared.

Artist Profiles

Craigie Aitchison

Born in Scotland in 1926, Craigie Aitchison spent much of his early life in Dunbartonshire. After initially undertaking studies in law, he opted for a career in art and studied at the Slade School of Art in London (1952–4).

In 1955 Aitchison won a scholarship to Italy and was greatly influenced by the Italian landscape, its quality of light and the simplistic representation of events and stories by Italian artists. Shortly after his return to London, he developed a style characterized by simple forms, strong almost luminescent colours and a freedom from extraneous details. His paintings are mostly portraits, or studies of figures, animals and plants, as well as still lives and crucifixions. His works are in many national and international collections including The Tate Gallery, London, the Scottish National Gallery of Modern Art, Edinburgh, and the Art Gallery of New South Wales, Sydney, Australia.

See illustration on page 56.

Peter Angermann

Born in Rehau in Bavaria in 1945, Angermann studied at the Akademie der Bildenden Kunst in Nuremberg (1966–8), and at the Kunstakademie Düsseldorf (1968–72). He founded the TIUP group with Robert Hartmann, Hans Rogalla and others, and later the NORMAL group with Milan Kunc and Jan Knap. Angermann worked in the U.S.A. (1982–3), and taught in Reykjavik and Kassel before returning to Nuremberg.

See illustration on page 58.

Lesley Banks

Born in Denny, Stirlingshire in 1962, Lesley Banks graduated from Glasgow School of Art in 1984. She won several national art awards and travelling scholarships and in 1989 left her part-time work as an assistant at Compass Gallery, Glasgow to paint full-time in her studio in the city's east end.

Her distinctive, figurative style has much popular appeal and she excels at injecting a hint of impending doom into an apparently normal, domestic setting. The enclosed space of Arlington swimming baths has provided the inspiration for one series of canvases. Other themes have derived from people, interiors or scenes she encountered while studying in Italy or holidaying in Cornwall. Her most recent paintings concerning her own pregnancy reflect a new interest in the unique moments before and after childbirth.

John Bellany

Born in the small fishing village of Port Seton, East Lothian, Scotland, in 1942, his father and both grandfathers were fishermen. He attended Edinburgh College of Art (1960–5), winning the Andrew Grant Scholarship (Paris 1962), and the Postgraduate Travelling Scholarship (Holland, Belgium 1965).

Bellany continued his studies at the Royal College of Art, London (1965–8) where he won the Burston Award. Later in the 1960s and 70s he held numerous part-time teaching posts in art colleges in England, but has always worked as a full-time artist.

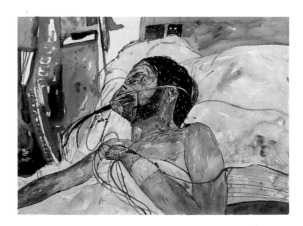

John Bellany
Self Portrait: Addenbrookes Hospital Series 1988
WATERCOLOUR OVER PENCIL
56 x 78cm

A Long Night's Journey into Day, an exhibition to mark his 50th birthday, was held at the Art Gallery and Museum, Glasgow (1992). His work is represented in major private and public collections including The Tate Gallery, London, the Contemporary Art Society, the National Gallery of Poland and the University of Western Australia, Perth.

See illustrations on pages 20, 54, 55.

Eduard Bersudsky

Born in Leningrad (now St Petersburg) in the former Soviet Union in 1939, Bersudsky made his living as a metal worker, electrician, watchman, ship's captain and stoker, and in the 1970s started making large wooden sculptures for gardens and parks. He also made his own private sculptures which he showed only to his friends.

In 1988 he met theatre director Tatiana Jakovskaia, and they opened the *Sharmanka* (barrel organ) Theatre in 1989. The mime artists who originally performed along with his sculptures were supplanted by the sculptures themselves which have many moving parts and are made of found materials. His wooden pieces owe a debt to Dutch street organs, which Bersudsky admires, while his metal constructions (*kinemats*) are inspired by Tinguely, and the whole performance recalls the fantasies of Hieronymus Bosch. Sound, movement, light and the casting of weird and wonderful shadows are vital elements in each work.

Eduard Bersudsky

Bersudsky and Jakovskaia have received encouragement and hospitality from Scottish woodcarver and furniture designer Tim Stead, and have recently set up their Theatre in King Street, Glasgow.

See illustrations on pages 49 and 50.

Elizabeth Blackadder

Born in Falkirk, Scotland, in 1931. After she graduated from Edinburgh University and College of Art, scholarships enabled her to travel and study in Greece, the former Yugoslavia and Italy. She married John Houston in 1956 and began teaching at Edinburgh College of Art where she remained until 1986. Travel abroad has provided much inspiration for her work, as have her garden and her cats. Elizabeth Blackadder's contribution to the world of art has been acknowledged by awards and honours, including the O.B.E. Her work has been widely exhibited and collected at home and abroad.

Elizabeth Blackadder
Waterlilies and Koi Carp 1993
WATERCOLOUR
173 x 183cm

Boyle Family

Mark Boyle	born 1934
Joan Hills	born 1936
Sebastian Boyle	born 1962
Georgia Boyle	born 1964

Mark Boyle, born in Glasgow, and Joan Hills, born in Edinburgh, met in 1956 and founded *The Institute of Contemporary Archaeology* and *The Sensual*

Laboratory. Their avant-garde activities have included theatrical events, body works and light environments for musicians such as Jimi Hendrix and *Soft Machine*.

Their *World Series* began in 1968; it is intended to consist of 1000 randomly selected 'earthprobes'. More recent works undertaken by the family involved their two children. Sites are chosen by throwing a dart at a map of the world, with the final plot determined by tossing a metal T-square into the air. Replication is then made of that section of the earth's surface by skilful, almost magical use of moulding and casting with fibreglass, sand, colouring, and found objects, etc. The resulting 'picture' is intended for display on a wall.

The family does not belong to any modern 'ism' although their work is analogous in some ways to photorealism. No personal style is imposed – 'We just do it', is their explanation.

See illustration on page 28.

lack of success with several London art galleries, Byrne started to produce paintings in a 'naif' style under the guise of his 72-year-old father, whom he claimed lived on a beach in Dunoon, west of Scotland. To his great surprise and amusement, the galleries responded with interest and 'Patrick' had a series of sell-out shows.

He currently lives in London and continues to work as an artist and writer. His work is represented in collections in the United Kingdom and abroad including Manchester City Art Gallery, the Fassler Collection, Hartford, Connecticut, U.S.A.. and the Lobel Gallery, Stockholm, Sweden.

See illustration on page 42.

John Byrne
Self Portrait in Stetson 1989
OIL ON CANVAS
90 x 70cm

Byrne had a pair of red braces and a stetson which were given to him as a present from an American actor in Kentucky in 1979. He felt that it 'seemed natural to put them together and do a self portrait as a cowpoke – a wry comment on how all Glaswegians imagine themselves as cowboys.' The work was painted while he was writing *Your Cheatin' Heart*.

Boyle Family with *Kerb Study* at the Art Gallery and Museum, Kelvingrove, Glasgow, in 1987

John Byrne

Born in Paisley, Scotland, in 1940, Byrne is a graduate of Glasgow School of Art and has a considerable reputation, not only as a painter and printmaker but also as an author of works, including *Writer's Cramp* (1977) and *The Slab Boys* (1978). As a writer Byrne is perhaps best known for his recent works for television – *Tutti Frutti* and *Your Cheatin' Heart* – which reflect his interest in popular music and humour.

Byrne's sense of humour as a painter can be seen in his adoption of the pseudonym 'Patrick'. Following a

Joyce Cairns

Born in Haddington, Scotland in 1947, Cairns trained at Gray's School of Art, Aberdeen, and The Royal College of Art, London, before postgraduate scholarships enabled her to travel and study abroad – particularly in Italy and the U.S.A. In 1967 she returned to Aberdeen as Lecturer in Drawing and Painting at Gray's School of Art. Joyce Cairns is a member of several art societies and in 1985 was elected first woman President of the Aberdeen Artist's Society. Her work has been widely exhibited and collected.

Joyce Cairns
TV Dinners 1991
OIL ON BOARD
214 x 245cm

TV Dinners was, says the artist, inspired by the Gulf War – 'eating food in front of the TV while all the horrors were displayed, the awful tabloids, and boats that were in turn sheds, missiles and coffins, set against the backcloth of the North Sea.'

Robert Campbell Jr

Born in Kempsey, in northern New South Wales in 1944, Robert Campbell Jr belonged to the Ngaku people. Although the tradition of their ancestors was rapidly dying out, Campbell spent his early years in an extended family living a settled, but nevertheless, Aboriginal lifestyle.

At primary school his first artistic endeavours were designs of kangaroos, birds and other animals which his father then incorporated on the surface of his hand-carved boomerangs.

Leaving school at the age of fourteen, Campbell continued to develop his gift using gloss paint and cardboard to paint bold naïve visions of the local landscape. He worked for a while in a series of menial jobs, as a factory hand in Sydney, as a labourer, as a pea-picker. As he put it, this was work 'that was not good enough for white people.' On his return to Kempsey he started to use canvas and artist's board for the first time. He recorded with sparkling vividness the scenes that he saw about him or that he remembered from his childhood. These works combine an uncompromising directness with a richness of colour and cartoon-like simplicity. They touch on themes of camp life, of food gathering and unspoilt nature but also of the darker side of twentieth-century Aboriginal life, of alcoholism, of police brutality and racism. Robert Campbell Jr died in 1993.

See illustration on page 30.

Steven Campbell

Born in Glasgow in 1953, Campbell spent seven years as a maintenance engineer and fitter in a steelworks (1970–7), before attending Glasgow School of Art (1978–82). In 1982 he was awarded a Fulbright Scholarship which enabled him to travel to New York, where he remained until 1986.

His work is represented in the collections of the Scottish Arts Council and the Contemporary Art Society, and in public collections in Edinburgh, Southampton, London (The Tate Gallery) and Liverpool. In the U.S.A. his work can be seen in the Art Institute, Chicago, Cincinnati Art Museum, Metropolitan Museum, New York, and the Walker Arts Center, Minneapolis.

See illustration on page 52.

Fionna Carlisle

Born in Wick, Caithness, Scotland, in 1954, Fionna Carlisle studied at Edinburgh College of Art (1972–6) and was awarded an Andrew Grant Postgraduate Scholarship (1976–7). In 1982 a Scottish Arts Council bursary allowed her to travel extensively in China, Thailand and Sri Lanka. Since then she has lived on the Greek island of Crete.

Major corporations including IBM, Coopers & Lybrand and Phillips Petroleum have purchased her work, which can also be seen at the Scottish Arts Council and Contemporary Art Society, and in public collections in Dundee, Edinburgh, Greenock, Motherwell, Leeds and Chelmsford.

She has exhibited at the Royal Scottish Academy, the Royal Society of Painters in Watercolour and the

Scottish Arts Council, and has participated in major group shows in London, Paris, Chicago, New York, Los Angeles, Moscow and Hong Kong.

Fionna Carlisle
Anterastes III 1986
ACRYLIC ON PAPER
199 x 202cm

Sir Anthony Caro
Table Piece Z85 'Tiptoe' 1982
RUSTED STEEL CONSTRUCTION
88 x 107 x 76cm

Over a hundred 'table pieces' were produced to complement his familiar floor pieces. Recent work has included examples of 'sculpitecture', a term devised to describe the fusion of architecture and sculpture, while Caro has also turned to using ceramics and even paper for some of his assemblages.

Sir Anthony Caro

Born in London in 1924, Anthony Caro studied engineering at Christ's College, Cambridge and sculpture at Regent Street Polytechnic and also at the Royal Academy Schools, London. He was part-time assistant to Henry Moore 1951–3 and taught at St Martin's School of Art, London 1952–79, apart from a period at Bennington College, Vermont, USA, 1963–5.

Caro's work of the fifties, modelled in clay or cast in bronze, was based on the figure, albeit expressionistically. By the time of his mould-breaking exhibition at the Whitechapel Gallery, London in 1963, he had fully developed his now familiar style of pure abstract metal forms, welded, riveted or bolted together and often painted in one, usually bright, colour. These highly influential pieces, inspired by American artists such as Richard Smith, were in tune with the rebellious sixties. They stamped him as one of Britain's most significant sculptors of the post-war era, and he has gone on to receive world acclaim. He was knighted in 1987.

Caro has continued to produce purely abstract assemblages which hark back at times to his early engineering training, although colour was gradually dispensed with through the seventies in favour of plain, varnished or rusted steel.

Henri Cartier-Bresson

Born in Chanteloupe, France in 1908, Henri Cartier-Bresson first took up photography in 1931 and became assistant director to the French film-maker Jean Renoir in 1936. He was a founder of the Magnum group which produced some of the strongest images in photo-reportage in post-war Europe.

Although Cartier-Bresson had been a prisoner of war between 1940–3, his own work tended to avoid graphic representations of conflict and focused instead on the way in which such large-scale events had an impact on people's everyday lives. Some of Cartier-Bresson's most famous photographs show his skill in capturing moments or actions in people's lives, and this enduring interest in humanity is vividly communicated by the emphasis he places on the human figure within his photographs.

See illustrations on pages 26 and 27.

Beryl Cook

Born in Surrey, England, in 1926, Beryl Cook has now settled in Devon with her husband John after having led a richly varied life. She began painting, originally for her own pleasure, while living in Southern Rhodesia (now Zimbabwe) and continued to build up a body of work after returning to England. She was first persuaded to show and sell her paintings in the mid 1970s, and since that time the popularity of her work has increased in leaps and bounds.

Important exhibitions include: Plymouth Arts Centre (1975); Whitechapel Gallery, London (1976); *Craft of Art*, Walker Art Gallery, Liverpool (1979); and a retrospective touring exhibition (1988–9).

See illustrations on pages 39 and 40.

Ken Currie

Born in North Shields, England, in 1960, Ken Currie trained at the Paisley College of Technology and Glasgow School of Art (1978–83).

His paintings are about the acutely troubled and disturbing times in which we live. His observations of the dark side of Glasgow life form the basis for much of his work, which explores poverty, isolation, madness and conflict within its social and political context. His compositions are often on a monumental scale.

Awards Currie has received include: the Newbery medal, Glasgow School of Art (1983); Elizabeth Greenshields Foundation Scholarship (1982); Cargill Scholarship, Glasgow School of Art (1983); and the Scottish Arts Council Young Artists Bursary (1985).

See illustrations on pages 16 and 23.

Ken Currie

Alan Davie

Born in Grangemouth, Scotland, in 1920, the son of a painter and etcher, Alan Davie studied at Edinburgh College of Art (1937–40), then served in the Royal Artillery (1940–6) where his chief concerns were writing poetry and playing jazz.

Awarded a travelling scholarship by Edinburgh College of Art, he visited France, Switzerland, Italy and Spain (1947–9). In Venice he met Peggy Guggenheim who purchased one of his paintings and introduced him to the work of the American Abstract Expressionists including Rothko, Motherwell and Pollock.

Poet, painter, musician and teacher, he is one of this century's most significant Scottish artists. His work is represented in international collections including The Tate Gallery, London, and the Museum of Modern Art, New York. Awarded the C.B.E. in 1972, he lives in Hertfordshire, Cornwall and St Lucia in the Caribbean.

In 1950 the first of many solo shows was held at Gimpel Fils Gallery, London. In 1958 Davie represented Britain at the Venice Biennale, and in 1963 was awarded the prize for best foreign painter at the VII Biennale in São Paolo, Brazil. He has had many solo exhibitions throughout the world and a major retrospective at the McLellan Galleries, Glasgow (1991).

See illustrations on 65 and 66.

Joe Davie

Born in Glasgow in 1965, Joe Davie is a graduate of Glasgow School of Art. With two friends he founded the Lighthouse Studio in Glasgow, their aim being to divide their time equally between painting and book illustration/design. Their premises were near Glasgow Print Studio and Davie soon became an expert printmaker; in 1990 he was selected by the Studio to take part in the Glasgow-Berlin Book Project. Since then, Davie has been working on images with a common theme.

Joe Davie
Apostleship 1991
OIL ON CANVAS
183 x 229cm

Originally inspired by Daniel Defoe's *A Journal of the Plague Year*, Davie has produced a whole series of prints and oil paintings to make up his *Journal of the Blackout*. Davie's characters include pilgrims, healers, monks and plague doctors who are modern apostles. Their mission is to bring light, hope and redemption to the dark places, hence the witty inclusion of electrical appliances and diagrams.

Francis Davison

Born in London in 1919, and brought up in France and England, Davison read English and Anthropology at Cambridge. He was always interested in drawing and painting and started painting seriously in 1947. In 1948 he married Margaret Mellis and went to live in the South of France. In 1950 they returned to England and settled in Suffolk where they worked a small-holding until 1954. He died in 1984.

By the early 1950s, Davison's paintings had become simplified into flattened shapes of colour, and by 1952 he had made his first collages. During the 1960s and 1970s, he introduced a wide range of colour and dispensed with any direct reference to landscape.

Davison is represented in the collections of The Tate Gallery, London, the Graves Art Gallery, Sheffield, and Manchester City Art Gallery.

See illustration on page 60.

Francis Davison

Ian Hamilton Finlay

Born in Nassau, Bahamas, in 1925 to Scottish parents, Ian Hamilton Finlay came to Scotland as a child. He did not complete any formal art training, although he attended Glasgow School of Art briefly before being called up to the armed forces, seeing service in

Germany. He took a variety of agricultural and labouring jobs after the war and began writing poems and plays. In 1961 he founded The Wild Hawthorn Press and was editor 1962–8 of its periodical *Poor. Old. Tired. Horse*. He moved with his wife Sue into an isolated farmhouse Stonypath, Dunsyre, Lanarkshire at the southern end of the Pentland Hills in 1966. Later re-named Little Sparta, the surrounding land was turned into a garden reflecting Finlay's intense interest in the Classical and Neo-Classical traditions; sculptures, many of them bearing inscribed allusions, are strategically placed in a natural setting. References to the French Revolution and Nazi symbolism abound in his *oeuvre* to indicate different extremes of terror.

Finlay's work is often made in close collaboration with a chosen artist, the result being of a characteristically clear-cut, crafted appearance. He cannot be easily defined as a visual poet or a conceptual artist, he describes himself simply as poet, artist, revolutionary. His huge and often controversial output includes sculptures, mostly in carved stone and wood, prints, cards, pamphlets and a variety of textual works on materials such as glass as well as the printed page. Landscape installations can be seen in several Continental countries and in America. He is well represented in art galleries throughout Europe and Britain.

See illustration on page 67.

Nikita Gashunin

Born in the former Soviet Union in 1956, Nikita Gashunin is one of a highly significant number of young Russian artists whose work is achieving acclaim on an international scale. He has exhibited in most of Moscow's major galleries, at the Biennale of

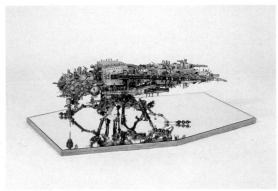

Nikita Gashunin
The Fly 1991
METAL ASSEMBLAGE
30 x 91 x 61cm

Contemporary Art, Leningrad (St Petersburg), and at the 1990 Exhibition of Soviet Contemporary Art in Tokyo. His work is also represented in several collections, including the Tretyakov State Gallery in Moscow. In 1992 he made a short visit to Scotland with his wife.

William Gear

Born in Methil, Fife, Scotland, in 1915, William Gear studied at Edinburgh College of Art and University and was briefly with Fernand Léger in Paris while on a travelling scholarship. After war service he lived in Paris 1947–50, mixing with abstract painters such as Hartung, de Staël and Soulages, and became part of the Cobra group (made up of members from Copenhagen, Brussels and Amsterdam) of which Karel Appel was the central figure.

He settled in London in 1950, joined the London Group in 1953, was Curator of the Towner Art Gallery, Eastbourne 1958–64 and Head of the Faculty of Fine Art, Birmingham University 1964–75.

William Gear
Summer Garden 1951
OIL ON CANVAS
122 x 81cm

One of the first Scottish artists to paint in a recognisably abstract style, he was readily accepted in exhibitions and public collections throughout the world, including showing alongside Jackson Pollock in New York in 1949. He had to wait much longer, however, for general acceptance in the country of his birth.

Andy Goldsworthy

Born in Cheshire, England, in 1956, Goldsworthy studied at Bradford Art College (1974–5) and Lancaster Art College (1975–8). He has lived in Yorkshire, Lancashire and Cumbria, slowly moving northwards until he settled in Dumfriesshire, Scotland, where he has remained for more than ten years.

Andy Goldsworthy
Overcast Cold/Upturned Leaves … Sidobre, 4 June 1989
PHOTOGRAPHIC PRINT
146 x 76cm

'The work explores not just the leaf, but also the space and light.

'Each leaf is held to the bracken with thorns, yet gives a feeling of travelling through the bracken rather than being attached to it. This is why it is linear rather than grouped. One leaf leads to another in a visual trail through the forest.

'The white undersides of the leaves were more apparent because of the windy overcast day. Had it been sunny, I may not have noticed the white – it would have been lost in the camouflaged, dappled forest light.

'Even so, I would not have made the work in any other light – it needed to be dark to make sense of the white. That it was windy not only revealed the white but also animated the line.'

Goldsworthy has exhibited in many countries including the U.S.A., France, Australia and Japan. Although his projects have taken him to far-off places, Goldsworthy retains a firm connection with his home which he feels is the main source of his work. He is regarded internationally as one of the leading artists dealing with the forms, processes and transformations in nature. He works with a myriad of natural materials, which he either uses directly or builds up into new forms; these have included leaves, stones, earth, snow and ice. The inevitable changes in these materials over time, as a result of changing temperatures, are integral parts of his work, and Goldsworthy documents these through the medium of photography.

His works are in the collections of Carlisle Museum and Art Gallery, Leeds City Art Galleries and the Henry Moore Centre for the Study of Sculpture, Yorkshire, the Scottish Arts Council, Fukuyama Museum of Art, Hiroshima, Japan and the Tochigi Prefectural Museum of Fine Arts, Utsonomiya, Japan.

Alexander Guy (also known as Sandy Guy)

Born in St Andrews, Scotland, in 1962, Guy studied at Duncan of Jordanstone College of Art, Dundee (1980–4), and at the Royal College of Art, London (1985–7). Since then he has had residencies at the Delfina Studios Trust, London, and with Susan Kasen Summer and Robert Summer, New York. He was a part-time tutor at Glasgow School of Art in 1963 and has recently been working in Glasgow and London.

See illustrations on pages 56 and 57.

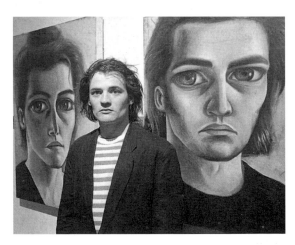

Alexander Guy
Photograph by David Mitchell

Andrew Hay

Born in Glasgow in 1944, Andrew Hay is a self-taught artist who left school at the age of fifteen with few formal qualifications. In 1987 he gave up his job as a lorry driver for the Co-op to concentrate on his painting full-time.

During Glasgow's Year of Culture in 1990, Hay occupied the post of artist-in-residence in several urban communities including Govan, Springburn and Easterhouse working in the libraries and in the Forge at Parkhead. Finding inspiration in the everyday lives of the local people, he produced a number of bold, powerful images which were exhibited at the Mitchell Library. Since then, Hay has strengthened his ties with community-based projects – conducting workshops in Elmvale, Glasgow, working with mentally handicapped adults and producing a huge composition on the Gulf War called *A New World Order* for Royston Hill Community Centre.

Andrew Hay
The Hierarchy of Art
OIL ON CANVAS
148 x 103cm

Hex

Founded in 1990, Hex is a collaboration of artists, designers, computer programmers, disc jockeys and music producers founded by Robert Pepperell and Matt Black. It includes the video graphic artists Hardwire, as well as the Coldcut re-mix act which had popular record hits with artists such as Yazz and Lisa Stansfield.

Drawing on a pool of talents and experience – including the set designs for films such as *Judge Dredd* and *Frankenstein* – Hex has produced a number of installations, exhibitions and films, in addition to commercially available software and interactive media for Phillips and Virgin. Hex has exhibited at the ICA and the London Film Festival.

'A lot of people are saying that the computer is the biggest thing since the wheel; I think the computer is the biggest thing since fire.

'It's an incredible feeling … painting with light on a computer screen for the first time. Everyone has beauty in them. I want them to be able to express it in a playful way. I want there to be more toys, software toys.'

Matt Black 1995

See illustration on page 63.

David Hockney

Born in Bradford, England in 1937, David Hockney studied at Bradford College of Art 1953–7 and the Royal College of Art, London 1959–62, where he made a name for himself as an unorthodox student. Since winning a junior painting prize at the John Moores exhibition, Liverpool, he has received a large number of awards and taken part in personal and group exhibitions all over the world.

His early semi-abstract expressionist, graffiti-inspired style of drawing and painting was changed into a more dead-pan figurative style by his experience of art in America, which he first visited in 1961. His subjects, too, are chosen to reflect the affluent and modish surroundings of California, in particular Los Angeles, where he now spends most of his time. He is now best known for his images of swimming pools beneath a clear sky, portraits of his parents, friends and lovers, book illustrations and homo-erotic subjects.

Designing sets and costumes for the stage has also featured prominently since 1966 and he has experimented with photography, creating composite, sometimes 3D arrangements.

David Hockney
An Illustration from 'Fourteen Poems by C. P. Cavafy'
1966
ETCHING
35 x 22cm

He is renowned for his mastery as a draughtsman, whether in pencil, pen or crayon, and consequently as a printmaker whose etchings and lithographs have ensured world-wide distribution of his work.

See illustration on page 8.

Oleg Holosiy

Born in Dniepropetrovsk, Ukraine, in 1965, Oleg Holosiy attended the art school in his home town. He graduated from there in 1984, and then from the Art Institute in Kiev in 1990. He became a member of the U.S.S.R. Artists' Union. He settled in Kiev and took part in successful exhibitions in the Ukraine, Russia and other parts of Europe. Holosiy died in tragic circumstances in 1993.

His large, freely painted canvases reveal an ever-changing imagination, a manifestation of what is called 'new expressionism'. Inexplicable dream-like episodes give way to scenes of horror and bestiality. Biblical and literary allusions, figures from a bygone age, often inspired by the paintings of earlier Russian artists, and animals from other continents are only a few of the many subjects tackled by Holosiy.

See illustration on page 51.

Dora Holzhandler

Dora Holzhandler was born in Paris in 1928 to Polish-Jewish immigrant parents. The family moved to London in 1933, but after the war she returned to Paris to study at the Sorbonne. Back in London she attended the Anglo-French Art Centre in St John's Wood, where she met her future husband, George Swinford. They raised a family of three daughters and have travelled extensively. Her work has been widely exhibited in Britain and abroad for many years and is represented in many public collections including St Mungo Museum of Religious Life and Art, Glasgow.

See illustration on page 35.

Dora Holzhandler

Peter Howson

Born in Isleworth, London, in 1958, Howson moved to Scotland in 1962, where he attended the Glasgow School of Art (1975–7), before abandoning his studies and taking various jobs – including a period in the Scottish infantry – and travelling in Europe. He returned to the Glasgow School of Art (1979–81) to study under Sandy Moffat, who in turn introduced him to the work of Otto Dix, Max Beckman and Fernand Léger.

In 1985 Howson was Artist-in-Residence at St Andrews and has also worked as a part-time tutor for the Glasgow School of Art. In 1993 he was commissioned by the Imperial War Museum, London, to visit Bosnia as a war artist. Following his first short,

traumatic visit and a second, less publicised one, Howson produced a major series of works which were exhibited in London in 1994.

His work is represented in major corporate and public collections throughout the United Kingdom and the U.S.A. His patrons include showbusiness personalities Madonna, Bob Geldof, Sylvester Stallone and Robbie Coltrane.

See illustrations on pages 17 and 18.

Patrick Hughes

Patrick Hughes was born in Birmingham, England, in 1939. His first solo exhibitions took place in 1961 at the Portal Gallery, London, and the King Street Gallery, Cambridge. Since then he has exhibited regularly in London, throughout the United Kingdom, the U.S.A. and Canada.

His works are represented in most of the major public collections in Britain. His publications include *Upon the Pun: Dual Meaning in Words and Pictures* (with P. Hammond), London (1978); *Vicious Circles and Infinity. An Anthology of Paradoxes* (with G. Brecht) New York (1979); *Behind the Rainbow* (with B. Smith), London (1983), and *More on Oxymoron*, London (1984).

See illustration on page 59.

Mathias Kauage

Kauage is a Chimbu from the Simbu Province in the Papua New Guinea Highlands. He only attended a Mission Primary School for two months, and worked

Mathias Kauage

mainly on plantations, and briefly as an office cleaner in the capital, Port Moresby, before his talent for drawing and painting was encouraged by Georgina Beier, at the Centre for New Guinea Cultures, in the University of Papua New Guinea.

His first solo exhibition of woodcuts was at the University in 1969, where he has since exhibited many times, both alone and with other contemporary New Guinea artists.

He is known for his vibrant 'naïve' depictions of modern technology and the clashes between traditional and urban life.

See illustrations on pages 32 and 33.

John Keane

Born in Hertfordshire, England, in 1954, Keane trained at Camberwell School of Art, London. His paintings typically exploit contemporary events – often involving conflict – to bold critical effect. The artist's point of view (both literal and metaphorical) nudges the viewer towards questioning motivations which lie behind desperate situations, as well as depicting their often ambiguous physical reality, both on the spot and in terms of media coverage.

John Keane was controversially appointed Official War Artist during the Gulf Conflict in 1991. His work has been widely exhibited, both in Britain and abroad, throughout his career.

John Keane
The Old Lie Café
OIL ON CANVAS
248 x 300cm

David Kemp

Born in London in 1945, Kemp spent four years in the Merchant Navy before studying at Farnham School of Art (1967–9), and Wimbledon Art School (1969–72). In 1973 he moved to West Cornwall.

His work consists mostly of assemblages from scrap materials, often made specifically for outdoor sites, such as land reclamation areas. He has had several residencies including those at the Grizedale Forest Park, Cumbria and the Yorkshire Sculpture Park, and has made over half a dozen sculptures, some on a vast scale, principally in Scotland, for Sustrans, the cycle path construction charity.

Exhibitions include: *White Man's Magic,* Graves Art Gallery, Sheffield and Drumcroon Gallery, Wigan (1983); *Out of Order*, McLellan Galleries, Glasgow (1991).

See illustration on page 48.

David Kemp

Peter Kennard

Born in London in 1949, Peter Kennard studied at the Slade School of Fine Art 1967–70 and at the Royal College of Art, London 1976–9.

Kennard's political photomontage works aim to emphasise such topics as the relationship between weapons research and the extremes of deprivation in the developing world. He is concerned with exposing invisible threats to society such as radioactive leakage and pollution, political indifference to the third-world economy and the disappearance of political prisoners. More recently Kennard has included object-based installations in his work, such as that produced for the Gimpel Fils Gallery in conjunction with his exhibition 'Images for the End of the Century' at the Imperial War Museum in 1990.

His work has been used by anti-nuclear, environmental and human rights campaigns; it has appeared on TV and in films, newspapers, on posters, tee-shirts, postcards and badges. It is included in collections at the Victoria and Albert Museum, the Imperial War Museum and the Saatchi Collection in London. His photomontages appear regularly in *The Guardian* newspaper.

Jack Knox

Born in Kirkintilloch near Glasgow in 1936, Jack Knox studied at Glasgow School of Art. In 1958 he won a travelling scholarship which enabled him to study in Paris where he worked in André L'hote's studio.

He then became impressed by the work of the American Abstract Expressionists, and his paintings of the mid sixties show their influence.

From this early style Knox moved through a period where his work related to the Pop Art movement and then he began to concentrate on still lifes of food and everyday objects using simplified forms and bright colour. By the early seventies these still lifes acquired a dramatic realism inspired directly by Dutch seventeenth-century art. His more recent landscapes and still lifes display an even bolder, more painterly quality.

Now retired, Knox was an influential teacher at Duncan of Jordanstone College of Art in Dundee and at Glasgow School of Art, where he was Head of Painting.

Jack Knox
Burning the Heather
OIL ON CANVAS
112 x 122cm

Bruce Lacey

Born in 1927, Lacey studied for six years at the Royal College of Art, London, and found work as a tap dancer, knife thrower, musician and prop-maker for the Goons. He currently lives on a farm in East Anglia, an environment which he finds inspirational – a 'magical place'.

Much of the power of his work comes from the way in which he uses disparate objects within his constructions, for example, the combination of mincers and dolls' heads. The links he perceives between unusual things provoke the viewer – often in a disturbing way – to consider these associations and their potential meanings.

Since the early 1960s Lacey has used a wide range of materials, including plastics, machine parts, robots and artificial limbs.

His work is represented in several public collections including The Tate Gallery, London. Lacey has exhibited in various shows and had a retrospective at the Whitechapel Art Gallery (1975).

See illustration on page 43.

Patricia Macdonald

Born in Edinburgh in 1945, Patricia Macdonald was educated at Edinburgh University, obtaining a BSc in 1967 and a PhD in Biological Science in 1973. She began her photographic training in her father's darkroom, following this with study and workshops with distinguished practitioners including John Blakemore, Thomas Joshua Cooper and David Williams.

An independent photographic artist and graphic designer, Macdonald was Head of Publications Design and Production for the National Museums of Scotland (1985–90). Much of her recent work has involved aerial photography, in collaboration with Angus Macdonald, Senior Lecturer in the Department of Architecture, Edinburgh University, as pilot and operations manager.

Her work is represented in many public and private collections, including the National Galleries of Scotland, the Scottish Arts Council and The Victoria and Albert Museum, London.

Macdonald has exhibited and published widely in Britain and abroad. Recent projects have included *Salt: Sand* Art Gallery and Museum, Kelvingrove, Glasgow in 1993.

Patricia Macdonald
Castle Island and Cracking Ice, Loch Leven 1987
CIBACHROME PHOTOGRAPHIC PRINT
40 x 59cm

'...there are various levels on which this photograph may be read. To those principally interested in factual description, the unusual patterns on the icy surface of the loch are significant. These were formed during a long period of extremely cold weather in the winter of 1986–7; such structures are normally only commonly found in polar regions.

'On another level, the picture is heavily symbolic, the imagery relating to the psychological power relations between the feminine and the masculine. This aspect of the picture is probably most clearly apparent to someone educated in Scotland and familiar with Castle Island as one of the most famous prisons, in the sixteenth century, of the unfortunate Mary, Queen of Scots.'

Jock McFadyen

Born in Paisley, Scotland, in 1950, McFadyen attended Saturday morning classes at Glasgow School of Art as a teenager. He studied at Chelsea School of Art, London (1973–7), and in 1981 he was the second

Jock McFadyen

artist-in-residence at The National Gallery, London. He later took up a part-time teaching post at the Slade School of Art while continuing to work at his studio in East London. In 1991 he was commissioned by the Imperial War Museum to record change in Berlin. Over the last five years he has spent part of the summer in his Edinburgh flat, seeking inspiration in far from fashionable areas, such as Granton, and the sleazy surroundings of some of the city's notorious 'go-go' pubs. McFadyen's distinctively expressive work is concerned with the so-called fag-end of society – spivs, drop-outs, glue sniffers, prostitutes, pimps and strippers. His Berlin visit saw him branch out into sculpture in a significant way for the first time.

He has exhibited widely in Britain; *Fragments from Berlin* was shown at the Imperial War Museum, London (1991), and a selection from it was exhibited at the Art Gallery and Museum, Kelvingrove, Glasgow (1992).

See illustration on page 41.

Keith McIntyre

Born in Edinburgh in 1959, Keith McIntyre was a student at Duncan of Jordanstone College of Art, Dundee. He has been associated with the trend for figurative painting which has dominated the work of younger Scottish artists since the mid eighties. He has also sought to maintain strong links with the community and has worked on several collaborative projects.

Public awareness of his art was firmly established by his huge theatrical backdrops for *Jock Tamson's Bairns* at the Tramway Theatre, Glasgow in 1990. His subsequent project, *Songs for the Falling Angel*,

Keith McIntyre
Psalms of the Shadows Opus II 1991
OIL ON CANVAS
274 X 184cm

explored the complex feelings and emotions aroused by the Lockerbie aeroplane bombing of 1988. He is currently a senior lecturer in painting at the University of Northumbria in Newcastle.

Bruce McLean

Born in Glasgow in 1944, McLean studied at the Glasgow School of Art (1961–3), before attending the advanced sculpture course at St Martin's School of Art, London (1963–6).

He worked in West Berlin on a DAAD fellowship (1981–2) and in 1985 won the John Moores Painting Prize. Described as having a schizoid attitude to the idiom he adopts, his work has been in sculpture, installation, performance art and stage design, and he has used painting, photography, ceramics and video. His work is frequently characterised by an unconventional and irreverent wit; he stated that the 'only way to see life is through humour. Humour is the nearest to truth that you can get.'

McLean's work is represented in major private and public collections throughout the world including the Scottish National Gallery of Modern Art, Edinburgh, The Tate Gallery, London, Van Abbemuseum, Eindhoven, The Netherlands, and the National Museum of Modern Art, Osaka, Japan.

He has exhibited and performed in Europe, the U.S.A. and Japan, and has taken part in major group exhibitions, including *A New Spirit in Painting*, London (1981); *Zeitgeist*, Berlin (1982); and *British Art in the 20th Century*, London (1987).

Bruce McLean
Untitled 1984
ACRYLIC, CHALK AND WAX ON CANVAS
two panels 210 x 334cm

John McLean

Born in Liverpool, England in 1939, John McLean attended the University of St Andrews (1957–62) and the Courtauld Institute of Art, London (1963–6). He then taught at the Chelsea School of Art and the Slade School of Art, London, and worked in New York. He currently lives and works in London.

McLean is one of the most prominent abstract artists now working in Britain. His sources of inspiration have come both from American colour field painting and the work of Henri Matisse and Joan Miro.

His work is included in the collections of the Arts Council of Great Britain, the British Council, the Scottish Arts Council, the Scottish National Gallery of Modern Art, Edinburgh, and The Tate Gallery, London.

McLean's exhibitions include those held at the Nicola Jacobs Gallery, London (1980 and 1983), *The British Art Show* (1980), the Scottish National Gallery of Modern Art (1989), and the Talbot Rice Art Gallery, Edinburgh.

See illustration on page 64.

John McLean
Photograph by Catherine Macavity

Will Maclean

Born in Inverness, Scotland, in 1941, Will Maclean studied at Gray's School of Art, Aberdeen. Following a postgraduate scholarship in 1966, he was awarded a travelling scholarship to Europe and studied at the

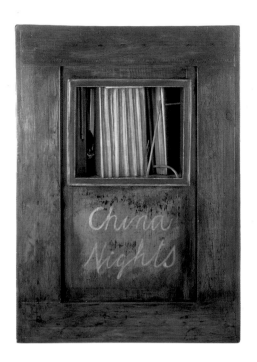

Will Maclean
China Nights 1983
MIXED MEDIA RELIEF
102 x 72 x 16cm

British School in Rome, and has been a Professional Member of the Society of Scottish Artists since 1968, and an Associate of the Royal Scottish Academy since 1978. He is presently based in Dundee where he is a lecturer at Duncan of Jordanstone College of Art.

His work is to be found in many British public collections. Exhibitions include *The Ring Net* solo exhibition, Glasgow, Edinburgh, Leeds, Campbeltown, Tarbet and Inverness (1978), The Düsseldorf Arts Fair (1983), and *Will Maclean*, Edinburgh and Glasgow (1992).

Michael McMillen

McMillen was born in Los Angeles in 1946. He lives with his wife in the house in Santa Monica where he was brought up by his grandparents. Taught to use hand tools by his grandfather, he subsequently learnt how to make objects, often from bits and pieces found in the neighbourhood. McMillen's father was a scenic designer who was fascinated by objects and the craft of illusion. Nearby Hollywood provided the young Michael with the magic of film sets and influenced his work.

He began his career in 1964 as an assemblage and installation artist, and also worked as a prop-maker for

Michael McMillen
Inner City 1977–9
MULTIMEDIA INSTALLATION
330 x 40 x 350cm

the films *Close Encounters of the Third Kind* and *Blade Runner*. His work is represented in the collections of the Guggenheim Museum, New York, the Los Angeles County Museum of Art and the National Gallery, Canberra, Australia.

David Measures

David Measures is an artist and teacher of art who has become increasingly interested in wildlife. He has taught in the Fine Arts Department of Nottingham

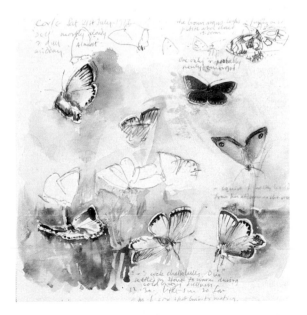

David Measures
Detail from *Butterfly Diary, 21 July 1973, Corfe*
WATERCOLOUR AND BIRO
35 x 17cm

Polytechnic, being concerned not only with art but also with music, drama and environmental studies. He took part in an acclaimed programme with David Bellamy entitled 'David's Meadow' which revolved around his work in a section of disused railway track near his home at Southwell, Nottinghamshire, which has become a superb piece of natural habitat with the passage of time. He is particularly interested in butterflies, which he has recorded in a series of illustrated diaries and has published a book on them *Bright Wings of Summer* (1976).

Margaret Mellis

Born in Wu-Kung-Fu, China, in 1914, Margaret Mellis came to Britain when she was one year old. She attended the Edinburgh College of Art (1929–33), winning a scholarship to study in Paris in 1933. After travelling in Spain and Italy, she returned to Edinburgh to take up a Fellowship (1935–7). Mellis then moved to London to work at the Euston Road School of Art and married the writer and painter Adrian Stokes. In 1939 they moved to St Ives in Cornwall. There she became part of the St Ives group of artists which included Barbara Hepworth, Ben Nicolson and Naum Gabo. Mellis continued to paint but also produced constructions of plywood, driftwood and found objects.

She later divorced Adrian Stokes and married Francis Davison in 1948. After two years in the South of France, they returned to England, and she has lived in Suffolk since his death in 1984.

Margaret Mellis in her studio
Reproduced by permission of *The Observer*

Her work is represented in many collections, including those of the The Tate Gallery, London, the Scottish National Gallery of Modern Art, and the Victoria and Albert Museum, London.

See illustration on page 61.

Lyndsay Bird Mpetyane

Lyndsay Bird Mpetyane was born in Ungoola, on the edge of the Simpson Desert in Eastern Central Australia, in about 1945. Having been forced to move several times because of drought, he and other members of his clan established a community at Mulga Bore, which followed a semi-traditional way of life, and where he is the senior law man.

The motivating force behind his production of art works for galleries and museums has its roots in the ceremonies which allowed the artist to acquire knowledge of ancestral designs and the skills to reproduce them. Lyndsay Bird Mpetyane's sense of design and colour, and his use of his particular medium, illustrate his enthusiasm for bridging the

Lyndsay Bird Mpetyane
Anarkakula 1993
ACRYLIC ON CANVAS
132 x 91cm

boundaries between western artists and the restricted domain of Aboriginal ceremonial art.

Pansy Napangati

Pansy Napangati was born at Hasst's Bluff, Australia, the daughter of a Walpiri tribesman and a Luritja tribeswoman, in the late 1940s.

The stories she depicts in her painting are based on the 'dreamings' of her mother and father's country

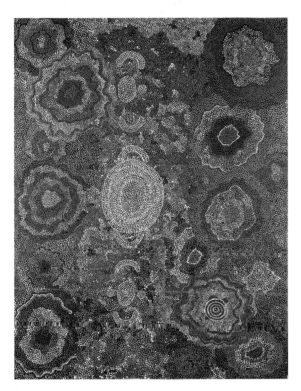

Pansy Napangati
Hailstorm Dreaming 1994
ACRYLIC ON CANVAS
128 x 97cm

'This painting shows the torrential rain of the rainy season. The vivid colours represent the fertility of the land now that the rains have replenished the earth. The rippled lines accentuated by a complex method of dotting show the water seeping into the earth and expanding underneath. The surrounding network of dotting depicts the ceremonial pathways that course across the land. In the centre of the painting is a Women's ceremony. The large yellow and white concentric circles in the centre indicate a sacred rock hole or campsite and women respectively. The ceremony could be celebrating an abundant food source as a result of the rains.'
(Information courtesy of the Rebecca Hossack Gallery, London).

which she learnt from fellow artists and family members. These included stories of Bush Banana, Water Snake, *Marlu* (kangaroo), Cockatoo, Bush Mangoes, Willy Wagtail, Seven Sisters, Hail, Desert Rain and *Kungkakutjara* (two women). She began to develop her own painting style during the 1960s while living at Papunya, and by the late 1980s she had emerged as Papunya Tula's foremost woman artist. In 1989 she won the sixth National Aboriginal Art Award.

Ron O'Donnell

Born in Stirling, Scotland, in 1952, Ron O'Donnell was a trainee photographer with Stirling University (1970–6) and studied photography at Napier College, Edinburgh (1970–3). In the late 1970s and early 1980s he began to photograph decaying interiors of buildings and by the mid 1980s had developed his own characteristic approach to his subject-matter. O'Donnell creates his own sets, usually by adapting existing settings, painting backgrounds, and adding objects that are often found in junkyards. His photographs are the finished works of art.

His works are included in major public collections, including those of the Scottish Arts Council and the Scottish National Gallery of Modern Art, Edinburgh. He has exhibited widely and was one of several photographers who attracted attention both nationally and internationally in the mid 1980s to contemporary Scottish photography. His work has been included in *Constructed Narratives: Photographs by Calum Colvin and Ron O'Donnell*, The Photographers Gallery, London (1968), *The Vigorous Imagination*, Scottish National Gallery of Modern Art, Edinburgh (1987), and *New Scottish Photography*, Scottish National Portrait Gallery, Edinburgh (1990).

See illustration on page 47.

Avril Paton

Born in Glasgow in 1941, Avril Paton is proud of her artistic heritage; both her late father, Hugh Paton, and grandfather, Donald Paton were painters from the Isle of Arran. With initial encouragement from her father she began to paint, eventually developing her own meticulously detailed style, using watercolour, sometimes with other media, where appropriate. Now based in the West End of Glasgow, she is best known for her ultra-realistic scenes from Glasgow life, but she also creates surreal poetic images based on her ties with Arran.

Avril Paton
Windows in the West 1993
WATERCOLOUR
122 x 152cm

Photograph courtesy of the artist

'On January 11th 1993 at about 5.30pm, there came a sudden heavy blizzard. In ten minutes it was over and the view from the attic window at Athole Gardens overlooking Saltoun Street was transformed. The lilac-pink sky, the lighted windows, the clarity of whiteness where there had been darkness – it was magical. By morning all the snow had gone, and the effect was never to be repeated during the mostly wild, wet winter.

'The building is uncommon in that many of the occupants work at home, often beyond office hours. That factor, combined with the goodly number of children, young persons and sociable adults living there, gives the place a distinctive appearance, particularly on a winter's evening before curtains are drawn and children sent to bed.

'With the memory still vivid, the first drawings were started in the middle of February and the painting completed at the end of June!'

Avril Paton

Sir Robin Philipson

Born in Broughton-in-Furness, Lancashire, England in 1916, Philipson completed his education in Dumfries, Scotland, before studying painting at Edinburgh College of Art (1936–40). After war service in India he returned to the staff of the College where he remained until his retirement as Head of the School of Drawing and Painting in 1982. He received many honours and served on a number of bodies in the art world, including Secretary (1969–71) and President (1973–83) of The Royal Scottish Academy. He was knighted for service to the arts in Scotland in 1976.

His paintings have been described as both expressionist and romantic, strongly influenced in the earlier years by Kokoschka whom Philipson admired. A number of themes which recur throughout his working life allowed him to give vent to his energetic and at times, highly coloured, approach: cockfights (recalling those he had seen in India), rose windows and church interiors, crucifixions, the First World War, black versus white, zebras and other African animals. He also continued to experiment with media, mixing polymers and collaged paper with oil and using glazes over his impasto to give added richness of effect. He died in Edinburgh in 1992.

Bridget Riley

Bridget Riley was born in London in 1931, and attended Goldsmith's College (1949–52) and the Royal College of Art (1952–5). She was influenced in early years by Neo-Impressionism and in particular by the paintings of Seurat. Riley's work is often referred to as Op Art which relies on the use of particular visual patterns and colours to create the impression of movement within the retina of the eye. It is, however, crucial to Riley that a work is always experienced as a whole, not just as a surface pattern. For her, painting is an all-consuming passion, endlessly presenting problems to be resolved. The process leading towards resolution – the finished work – can be a lengthy one and is often achieved through trial and error.

She has made a vital contribution to British abstract painting and became internationally renowned in the 1960s through her black and white 'optical' paintings. She was awarded the International Prize for Painting at the Venice Biennale in 1968. Inspired by her visits abroad, she began to create works using strong colours.

Her work is represented in many collections including The Tate Gallery, London, Museum of Modern Art, New York, Stedelijk Museum, Amsterdam, National Gallery, Berlin, and the National Museum of Modern Art, Tokyo, Japan.

See illustrations on pages 22 and 62.

James Robertson

Born in Cowdenbeath, Fife, Scotland in 1931, James Robertson studied at Glasgow School of Art where he is at present Senior Lecturer in Drawing and Painting.

His vivid, semi-abstract, landscapes which resound with rich colour and surface pattern have received much acclaim. He is represented in a large number of public and private collections including those of HRH Prince Philip and HM The Queen Mother.

Niki de Saint-Phalle

Catherine Marie-Agnès Fal de Saint-Phalle – known from childhood as Niki – was born near Paris in 1930 just as her father, then manager of the New York branch of the family banking house, lost his business and his entire fortune. The family moved to the U.S.A. where Niki, expelled from various convent schools, realized that she felt trapped by the conventional expectations about a woman's role in life.

She worked briefly as a model, before eloping at the age of eighteen with Henry Matthews, a U.S. marine and aspiring musician and poet. While he studied at Harvard, she began her first paintings. They moved to Paris and then travelled in Europe, but in 1953 she suffered a nervous breakdown as a result of struggling with the conflicting demands of a family and her own artistic freedom. By 1961 Niki had left her husband and children to concentrate on her art, and began her association with Jean Tinguely. Her major work during the last decade has been the vast *Tarot Garden* at Garavicchio, Tuscany.

Her work is represented in major public and private collections throughout the world. She has exhibited extensively in Europe, the U.S.A. and Japan. In 1993 a major retrospective of her work was seen in Bonn, Paris and the McLellan Galleries, Glasgow.

See illustration on page 46

Sebastião Salgado

Born in Brazil in 1944, Salgado trained as an economist, and moved to Paris in 1969. He became a professional photographer in 1973 and joined the famous Magnum Agency. He is now one of the world's leading photo-journalists, combining coverage of news events with more personal in-depth projects.

Salgado has been awarded almost every major photographic prize including Photographer of the Year and Photojournalist of the Year and has exhibited internationally in many venues. His current project concerns the migration of peoples across the world and is scheduled to be completed by the year 2000.

See illustrations on pages 24 and 25.

Michael Sandle

Michael Sandle was born in Weymouth, England, in 1936. He attended the Douglas School of Art and Technology on the Isle of Man (1951–4), completed two years of National Service in the Royal Artillery and studied printmaking at the Slade School of Art, London (1956–9). From 1962 he lectured at various art schools in Britain and Canada, moved to Germany in 1973, and taught at the Fachhochschule für Gestaltung, Pforzheim. In 1980 he became Professor at the Akademie der Bildenden Kunste, Karlsruhe, and continues to teach there.

Unlike most of his contemporaries in the 1960s, Sandle developed an interest in nineteenth-century figurative sculpture and public monuments, not only for their scale and public presence but also for their communicative power. His own 'monuments' do not glorify events; his stance is anti-authoritarian, pointing to the futility of war and man's abuse of power.

His work is represented in major collections, including the Australian National Museum, Canberra, the Hakone Art Museum, Japan, and the Imperial War Museum and the Victoria and Albert Museum, London.

Michael Sandle
A Mighty Blow for Freedom: Fuck the Media 1988
BRONZE, EDITION OF THREE
302 x 132 x 221cm

Duncan Shanks

Born in Airdrie, near Glasgow in 1937, Duncan Shanks studied at Glasgow School of Art under William and Mary Armour, David Donaldson and Geoffrey Squire, winning a travelling scholarship to Italy. He later returned as a part-time lecturer until 1979 when he left to devote all his time to painting. He is a member of the Royal Glasgow Institute of the Fine Arts, of The Royal Scottish Academy and the Royal Scottish Society of Painters in Watercolours and is represented in a large number of British public collections.

His chosen themes of landscape and still life take nature as a starting-point and then evolve into an expressionistic, semi-abstract image, achieved with sweeping brushstrokes of rich, vibrant colour. The landscape of the Clyde Valley near Lanark, where he lives, and the changing Scottish weather are his chief influences and he also derives inspiration from artists such as Samuel Palmer, Bonnard, Soutine, de Kooning and Alan Davie.

Paddy Japaljarri Sims

Born in 1916, Paddy Japaljarri Sims works from the Aboriginal community of 800 Warlpiri people at Yuendumu, north east of Alice Springs, Australia. The community is serviced by the Walukurlangu Aboriginal Artists Association which employs advisers to liaise between the hundred or so artists who work there and major national and international museums and galleries. Sims has collaborated with other artists in the production of large canvases, and his work has been shown in the Georges Pompidou Centre, Paris, and is held in the collection of the National Gallery of Australia, Canberra.

See illustration on page 29.

Hong Song-Dam

Born on an island off the south coast of Korea in 1955, Hong Song-Dam was the son of a schoolteacher and, although very poor, studied fine art at the University in Kwangju. He rejected the Western-oriented education he received, turning instead to traditional Korean media such as woodblock printing and large painted wall hangings, so that he could communicate better with the people of his country.

He became Director of the Kwangju Visual Arts Research Institute, championing the cause of the poor and oppressed, for which he was arrested and jailed in February 1990 for seven years; his sentence was later reduced to three years.

Most of his banners and prints were destroyed at the time of his arrest, but a series of woodcuts recalling the people's uprising in Kwangju in 1980 and produced in 1980–9, survived, and was bought by Glasgow Museums. He was adopted by Amnesty International as a Prisoner of Conscience.

See illustration on page 31.

Jo Spence

Jo Spence was born in London in 1934 and died in 1992. Artist and phototherapist, she encountered photography first in the 1950s and 60s. She opened a commercial studio in 1967 and embarked on a series of radical photographic projects (1973–5). In 1974 she formed the Photography Workshop with Terry Dennett and they produced the seminal *Photography/Politics One* (1979). She moved from a traditional, socialist-realist approach to one where she became the subject of each picture, acting and re-enacting various roles and subverting many of society's assumptions, sometimes with humour and sometimes in a very candid, emotional way. She developed breast cancer in the early 1980s and found herself in conflict with the health industry. In 1984 she invented Photo Therapy with Rosy Martin, combining elements of photography and psychotherapy.

Until her death in 1992, she continued to produce a series of writings, films and photographic projects that confront class, gender and power relationships, through reclaiming her body, her history and her right to disidentify herself from the roles that capitalism created for her.

See illustrations on pages 44 and 45.

Alexander Stoddart

Alexander Stoddart was born in Edinburgh in 1959, educated in Paisley, and studied at the Glasgow School of Art (1976–80). He entered Glasgow University to research the history of public sculpture and set up a workshop in Paisley. He worked for Ian Hamilton Finlay (1983–8), and then embarked on a series of large-scale architectural sculpture schemes for urban environments, including those for the Italian Centre and the Athenaeum, Glasgow.

Four massive 'keystone' projects are in progress, all monuments in praise of famous Scotsmen: Burns and Wilson (Kilmarnock), Hume (Edinburgh), Robert Adam (Glasgow) and James IV (Stirling).

Although at first glance it seems neo-classical, Alexander Stoddart characterizes his work as 'executed in that stylistic mixture involving neo-classicism, romanticism and realism, which mixture is effectual in the art of nation-building and highlights the truth of propaganda.'

Biederlally commemorates Councillor Pat Lally's action, in 1990, while chairman of the Glasgow Royal Concert Hall Board, in rejecting the modernist murals by Ian McCulloch which had been presented at the

Alexander Stoddart
Biederlally 1992
DEMOCRITITE (FIBREGLASS/POLYMER LAMINATE)
347 x 69 x 42cm

awarded a Commendation of Merit, Robert Colquhoun Memorial Exhibition and was short-listed for the Lord Provost's Prize. He lives and works in Glasgow where he is a Chief Instructor and Examiner for the Korean art of unarmed combat, *tae kwan do*.

Since his first solo exhibition at Rozelle House, Ayr (1977), he has had many solo shows throughout Scotland and in Blackpool, Chicago and Penang, Malaysia. He has exhibited at the Royal Scottish Academy, Edinburgh, and the Royal Glasgow Institute, and has participated in major group exhibitions throughout the United Kingdom and in Paris, Chicago, New York, Santa Fe, New Mexico and Hong Kong.

See illustrations on pages 68 and 69.

Victor Tiede

Born in Regina, Saskatchewan, Canada, in 1955, Victor Tiede began by working as a professional carpenter and furniture restorer, gaining his experience and knowledge of wood carving from repairing Victorian oak furniture. Since 1982 he has devoted more and more time to carving, and in 1987 began making art works full time. He became a carving instructor at the Rainbow Youth Center and then a woodwork shop supervisor at the Neil Balkwell Civic

opening. The outrage of the art world was summed up by the critic Clare Henry, who poured scorn on Lally's aesthetic sense, claiming in an article in *The Herald*:

'A mural of floral bouquets, pastoral sheperdesses and blue birds singing in an azure sky would perhaps have satisfied Lally.'

The scene Henry describes is like a Biedermeier picture – a stylistic term for a straightforward type of painting or furniture produced in nineteenth-century Germany.

Henry's taunts are translated into German and inscribed on the monument. Lally appears as the champion of plain, honest straightforward art, mounted on a classical post known as a herm. 'Herms usually appear on roadways: this one appears in the motorway out of Modernism', observes Stoddart.

Hock-Aun Teh

Hock-Aun Teh was born in Sungai Gedong, Western Malaysia, in 1950, and studied at the Tan Guan-Hin Chinese Painting School (1966–70) before attending Glasgow School of Art (1970–4). He has lectured on Chinese painting and calligraphy at Glasgow School of Art and for the Scottish Arts Council. In 1980 he was

Victor Tiede
How the West was Wild 1992
POLYCHROME WOOD
115 x 89 x 98cm

Arts Center. He has had a solo exhibition at the Prairie Gallery, Alberta, Canada, and has taken part in many group shows in Saskatchewan, Vancouver and Chicago.

Victor Vasarely

Born in Pecs, Hungary in 1908, Victor Vasarely abandoned his medical studies in Budapest in favour of art, attending the Poldini-Volkmann Academy of Painting 1925–7 and the Mühely Academy 1929–30, where he was introduced to the ideas of the Bauhaus. In 1930 he emigrated to France (being naturalised in 1959) and worked in Paris as an independent graphic artist, producing geometric fabric designs and advertisements for the pharmaceutical industry. He did chequerboard pattern and axonometric-perspective drawings at this time, but his first paintings date from 1944 when he helped Denise René to establish her Paris Gallery, where he has exhibited regularly since.

His interest in movement in art led to 3d experiments with perspex and his association with kinetic artists such as Calder, Duchamp and Tinguely. He is acknowledged as the originator of Op Art (a term first applied in 1965) and is hugely influential and successful, employing teams of assistants to execute his paintings, prints and sculptures in large multiple editions. The Vasarely Foundation at Aix-en-Provence was opened in 1976 to explore the artist's theories of urban development. The Vasarely Museum in his birthplace at Pecs was opened in 1976 and the Vasarely Centres in New York in 1978 and in Oslo in 1982. He lives at Annet-sur-Marne, France.

Nick Waplington

Born in Scunthorpe, England, in 1965, Nick Waplington studied at Worthing Art College, at Trent Polytechnic, Nottingham (1986–9) and the Royal College of Art (1989–92). He received Kodak British and European Awards in 1990 and the ICP New York Photographers Award in 1993.

While studying for his degree Nick Waplington began to photograph friends and neighbours on the estate on the outskirts of Nottingham where he lived with his grandfather. The first stage of the work appeared as the book *Living Room* in 1991. It is an ongoing project dealing with the time he spent with his friends and he hopes to continue the work indefinitely.

His is regarded as one of today's major photographic talents and has found notable supporters, not least Richard Avedon, who has publicly expressed his admiration for Waplington's pictures.

See illustration on page 37.

Paul Waplington

Born in Nottingham, England, in 1938, Paul Waplington trained as a lace draughtsman on leaving school and began painting in his spare time while working his way around Europe some years later. From 1965 he worked as a self-employed designer and draughtsman, but gradually his painting became his main activity. He exhibited widely and received various commissions. In 1983 he moved to Portugal.

See illustration on pages 36–7.

Alison Watt

Born in Greenock, Scotland in 1965, Alison Watt studied at Glasgow School of Art and, while still a student, won a number of prizes including the prestigious John Player Portrait Award. This led to a commission to paint HM The Queen Mother and the resulting portrait is now in the National Portrait Gallery, London.

Alison Watt
Marat and the Fishes 1990
OIL ON CANVAS
152 x 122cm

Influenced partly by James Cowie (1886–1956), the foremost Scottish figurative painter of his generation, Watt's portraits and figure paintings are carefully composed and meticulously drawn. To this technical accomplishment her cool colours and calm poses add a feeling of serenity which is sometimes further enhanced by an air of mystery or a touch of humour. Favourite motifs are kitchen objects – teacups, bowls, jugs – as well as water containers such as baths and tin tubs. Many of the subjects look like Watt herself and her most recent monumental triptychs have a personal symbolism which is extremely intriguing.

Adrian Wiszniewski

Adrian Wiszniewski was born in Glasgow in 1958 of Polish extraction. He studied at the Mackintosh School of Architecture (1975–9) before attending the Glasgow School of Art (1979–83), where he was a fellow student of Steven Campbell, Ken Currie and Peter Howson. The Cargill Scholarship in 1983 enabled him to travel to Paris, and a grant from the Mark Rothko Memorial Trust Fund in 1984 meant he could go to New York.

By 1985 his work had been purchased for The Tate Gallery, London and the Museum of Modern Art, New York. Other collections his work is represented in include the Scottish National Gallery of Modern Art, Edinburgh, the Walker Art Center, Minneapolis, the Gulbenkian Museum, Lisbon, Portugal and the Setagage Art Museum, Tokyo, Japan.

In 1991 his installation *The Secret Garden* was created for the Art Gallery and Museum, Kelvingrove, Glasgow.

See illustration on page 53.

Index